Differentiated
Projects
for Gifted Students

Grades 3–5

Differentiated Projects
for Gifted Students

Brenda Holt McGee
& Debbie Triska Keiser

PRUFROCK PRESS INC.
WACO, TEXAS

Prufrock Press Inc.
P.O. Box 8813
Waco, TX 76714-8813
Phone: (800) 998-2208
Fax: (800) 240-0333
http://www.prufrock.com

Table of Contents

Introduction

Differentiated Projects for Gifted Students was written to help teachers in third, fourth, and fifth grades differentiate instruction for advanced and gifted learners. The activities are hands-on, discovery-based, research-oriented, and cross-curricular. The content of the activities in *Differentiated Projects for Gifted Students* is based on social studies and science Common Core State Standards and national standards for third, fourth, and fifth grades. Math, language arts, and reading activities are integrated throughout.

How to Use This Book

Activities in *Differentiated Projects for Gifted Students* are grouped into chapters according to social studies and science standards. These activities can be assigned as independent study projects or can be completed by groups of students.

The activities in this book were written to support and extend instruction in upper elementary classrooms. When teachers are implementing units in social studies or science, they can choose extension activities to help students delve more deeply into subject matter.

The teacher may choose to use the activities in this book with all students. Some students may need more support with the research portions of these activities. In order to provide this extra support, we suggest bookmarking suitable websites in advance and enlisting the help of the library media specialist to gather print and electronic materials that students can use in the classroom.

Chapter 1
Energy Projects

Can You See Sound?

Materials Needed:

- Sound Experiment sheets (pp. 2–3)
- Overhead projector
- Tuning fork (borrow from music teacher)
- Transparent glass bowl
- Water
- Grains of rice
- Paper plate
- Computer with Internet access

Steps:

1. Use your favorite Internet search engine to research sound and answer the following questions:
   a. What is sound?
   b. How do our vocal cords work?
   c. How does sound register in our brains?
   d. What is the speed of sound?
   e. What is pitch?

2. Follow the directions on the Sound Experiment sheets to learn more about sound and to create a demonstration of how sound works.
3. Ask your teacher to set a time for you to share what you have learned about sound with the class.

Sound Experiment 1

Materials Needed:

- Overhead projector
- Tuning fork (borrow from music teacher)
- Transparent glass bowl
- Water

Steps:

1. Turn on the overhead projector and point it toward a wall. Place a glass bowl on the glass plate of the projector and add water. Allow the water to settle.
2. Strike the tuning fork on the floor, then touch it to the surface of the water.
3. Draw a picture of what you see. This is what sound waves would look like if we could see them.
4. Strike the tuning fork on the floor again. Place one end of the tuning fork on your ear lobe. Can you feel the sound waves transferring to your ear?

Sound Experiment 2

Materials Needed:

- Tuning fork (borrow from music teacher)
- Grains of rice
- Paper plate

Steps:

1. Place six grains of rice on the paper plate.
2. Strike the tuning fork on the floor and gently touch the tuning fork to the paper plate. What happens to the rice?
3. Repeat the experiment, this time placing the tuning fork firmly on the paper plate. How is the outcome different?

Sound Experiment 3

Materials Needed:

- Computer with Internet access
- Materials needed for your demonstration

Steps:

1. Using what you have learned about sound from the Internet and the experiments, create another experiment or demonstration to teach what you have learned to others.
2. If you create an experiment, be sure to list the materials needed and to record each step in the process as precisely as you can.

Magnetic Attraction

||||||||||||||||||||||||||||||||||||||||||||||||||||||||||||||||||||||||||||||||||||||||||||||||||||||||||||||||||

Grade Levels: 3–4

Materials Needed:

- 1 large bar magnet
- 1 iron nail
- 1 paperclip
- 1 container of iron filings
- 1 quart-sized plastic zipper bag
- 5 ring magnets
- Piece of white paper
- Hard object
- Pencil

Steps:

1. Create your own magnet by placing the pointed end of the nail on top of the bar magnet for several minutes. Test the strength of the new magnet by touching the tip of the nail to the paperclip. If the nail attracts the paperclip, you have created a magnet.
2. Magnets lose their magnetic abilities if they are dropped too often. Place the nail on the floor and hit it several times with a hard object. Test the nail again. You should notice a decrease in magnetism. This is why it is important not to drop magnets on the floor.
3. Stick the pencil eraser through each of the ring magnets. Arrange the magnets so that they float on top of one another. Discuss with a friend why you think this happens.
4. Pour the iron filings into the zipper bag and seal the bag. Lay the bag on a piece of white paper and shake it until the filings are evenly distributed. Slide the bar magnet under the paper and bag. Draw a picture of the results. The iron filings are showing you the magnetic field of the bar magnet.
5. Repeat Step 4 of the experiment with one of the ring magnets.
6. Write a paragraph describing the similarities and differences in the magnetic fields of bar and ring magnets, and explain why the ring magnets "floated" on the pencil. Share your findings with your group.

Let There Be Light!

Materials Needed:

- A variety of batteries (round watch battery, AA, AAA, C, D, 9-volt)
- 1 set of holiday lights (cut apart so that each light has two wires coming from it—have an adult help you use a wire stripper to expose the wires coming from each bulb)
- Paper
- Markers
- Flashlight

Steps:

1. Experiment with lighting the bulbs by placing one end of a holiday light wire to the positive side of a battery and the other end to the negative side of the same battery. Can you get a bulb to light with each of the batteries?
2. Twist two lights together to form a chain. Repeat Step 1 using two lights. Were you able to get both lights to light using each kind of battery?
3. Repeat the experiment with three lights twisted together.
4. Repeat Step 1, but this time, keep track of the brightness of the holiday light. Arrange the batteries in order from "produces brightest light" to "produces little or no light."
5. Create a bar graph and graph the batteries by the amount of light each produced.
6. At home, locate several flashlights. Open the flashlights and record the kind and number of batteries it takes to power each one. Create a chart with a description or picture of each flashlight that includes this information.
7. Using what you have learned about the strength of different kinds of batteries from experiments and observations, write an essay explaining why you think some electronic devices need smaller/larger batteries than others.

Conductors and Insulators

Materials Needed:

- 1 set of holiday lights (cut apart so that each light has two wires coming from it)
- 1 9-volt battery
- A small piece of wire
- Duct tape
- Items to test such as a penny, nickel, nail, marble, or thumbtack

Steps:

1. Create a circuit like the one shown in the picture using one holiday light, a 9-volt battery, duct tape, and a small piece of wire.

2. Test a variety of items from the classroom to discover whether they are conductors or insulators by touching both ends of the wire to the object. A conductor is a material that allows electricity to flow through it. An insulator does not allow electricity to flow through it.

3. Create a chart listing each item tested, whether the circuit was completed during each test (did the bulb light?), and whether each item was a conductor or an insulator.

4. Write a paragraph telling the differences between the two groups of objects. Be sure your concluding statement explains the difference between conductors and insulators.

5. Ask your teacher to plan a time for you to share your findings with the class.

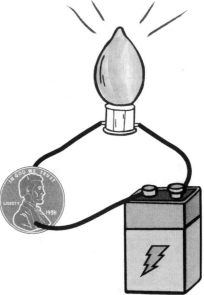

Chapter 2

Economics Projects

Wants and Needs

Materials Needed:

- Poster board
- Markers
- Library access or computer with Internet access

Steps:

1. Understand and define the difference between wants and needs.
2. Take a survey of all of the students in your class to come up with their top three wants and top three needs.
3. Research children's wants and needs in three developing countries like Somalia, Yemen, and Ethiopia.
4. Develop a list of what you think the top three wants and needs are in those countries.
5. Create a poster that compares what you found in your class with what you found in other countries.
6. Ask your teacher if you can explain and display your poster.

Careful Consumers

Grade Levels: 3–4

Materials Needed:

- None

Steps:

1. Think of a time when you were anxious and excited about getting a game or toy you saw advertised on television or in a toy store.
2. Ask yourself if you were ever disappointed with the product or toy once it was out of the box and you could see what was included and what it could do.
3. Imagine you were explaining to a younger group of children what lesson you learned from your experience and what they should look for in order to not make the same mistake.
4. Use this lesson to write a speech or talk you would give to these young children to teach them to be careful consumers.

How Do They Do It?

Materials Needed:

- Computer with Internet or library access

Steps:

1. Did you know that most products are made with a number of steps and a number of workers in an assembly line? Research a product that interests you like baseballs, action figures, dolls, or lollipops to determine how it's made.
2. Draw a diagram or flow chart of the steps that it takes to produce one of these products.
3. Brainstorm, then record a list of the pros and cons of working on an assembly line.
4. Share your findings with the class.

It's All in the Advertising

Grade Levels: 3–4

Materials Needed:

- Newspapers or magazines
- 1 copy of Advertisement Critic's Review Form (p. 11)

Steps:

1. Look at a newspaper or magazine for advertisements of products that might interest you.
2. Ask permission to cut out advertisements.
3. Select three advertisements and cut them out.
4. Staple one Advertisement Critic's Review Form to each advertisement.
5. Rate each advertisement using the criteria on the form.

Advertisement Critic's Review Form

Directions: Use the criteria on this form to critique each advertisement.

Describe and rate this advertisement based on the following scale:

      3: Very Effective   2: Good   1: Not Effective

Description of Advertisement	Layout (How the Ad Looked)	Copy (Words and Print)	Graphics (Artwork)	Overall Rating

Describe and rate this advertisement based on the following scale:

      3: Very Effective   2: Good   1: Not Effective

Description of Advertisement	Layout (How the Ad Looked)	Copy (Words and Print)	Graphics (Artwork)	Overall Rating

Describe and rate this advertisement based on the following scale:

      3: Very Effective   2: Good   1: Not Effective

Description of Advertisement	Layout (How the Ad Looked)	Copy (Words and Print)	Graphics (Artwork)	Overall Rating

Dependence on Oil

||||||||||||||||||||||||||||||||||||||||||||||||||||||||||||||||||||||||||||||||||||||||||||||||||||||||||||

Grade Levels: 4–5

Materials Needed:

- Computer with Internet access

Steps:

1. Use your favorite Internet search engine to research how much the United States depends on imports of crude oil from other countries.
2. Create a graph that shows whether the United States' oil imports have increased or decreased over the past 10 years.
3. Create a chart that shows the top five places where the United States gets its imported crude oil.
4. Write a summary that includes facts and your prediction about future crude oil imports to the United States. Be sure to include your opinion about the problems the U.S. might face as a result of your predictions.
5. Ask your teacher to find a time for you to present your findings to the class.

Cause and Effect

Grade Levels: 4–5

Materials Needed:

- Computer with Internet access

Steps:

1. Research the locations of the top five natural disasters between 1850 and 1950. For example, you might find the San Francisco earthquake of 1906.
2. Select one of these locations to do an in-depth research study on the immediate and long-term effects that the disaster had on the economics of the city, town, region, or country where it occurred.
3. Create your own graphic organizer to show the data you collected. Include several statistics like population, exports and imports, natural resources, and so on.
4. Determine what your location was like before and after the disaster. Was the area forever changed by the disaster?
5. Present your information in a creative way such as with a play, PowerPoint presentation, videotaped newscast, diorama, or poster.

Trickle-Down Debate

Grade Levels: 4–5

Materials Needed:

- Computer with Internet access

Steps:

1. Use your favorite Internet search engine to help you research the parts of a debate. Be sure to define the following parts: affirmative side, negative side, moderator, opening, first rebuttal, second rebuttal, and closing.
2. Define trickle-down economics or trickle-down theory. Try to answer the following questions as you research:
   a. Who coined the phrase "trickle-down economy"?
   b. What is it? Who would/did it benefit?
   c. What are the pros to a trickle-down economy?
   d. What are the cons to a trickle-down economy?

3. Prepare a scripted debate that argues for or against the theory of trickle-down economics. Be sure to write the opening arguments, first rebuttal, second rebuttal, and closing arguments for each side. You can use a search engine to look for sample debate scripts to help you get started.
4. Ask two classmates to rehearse the scripted debate you wrote.
5. Ask your teacher when you and your classmates can present the debate to the class.

Made in America

Grade Levels: 4–5

Materials Needed:

- Computer with Internet access

Steps:

1. Think about all of the products the United States imports. What do you think would happen if the U.S. suddenly banned all imports? Write a paragraph telling how you think you would be affected if all imports stopped.
2. Consider the economy of the United States if imports were stopped. What might happen if U.S. citizens could only buy products made in America? Create a chart listing 20 items in your locker or classroom and identify where these products were made. Were more items made inside or outside of the United States?
3. Identify at least five products Americans would be unable to make or buy without imports.
4. Many products are not made in America anymore because the cost of labor to make them is too expensive. Many companies have products made in foreign countries because they do not have to pay the people who make the products as much money to work. Identify at least five products you think Americans might not be able to buy because the cost of American labor would make the products too expensive.
5. Create a Glogster mash-up of photographs or a video newscast to show the results of your research. Your report should also include a persuasive conclusion on whether or not you would support stopping imports.

Chapter 3
Science Careers Projects

Volcanologist: An Explosive Career

Grade Levels: 3–4

Materials Needed:

- 1 large sheet of construction paper
- Computer with Internet access

Steps:

1. Use the Internet to discover what volcanologists do. Take notes about what you find.
2. Answer the following questions as you read about volcanologists:
   a. What is the major field of study for volcanologists in college? What degree do they earn? Is earning a Bachelor of Science (BS) degree enough?
   b. What kinds of classes can students take in high school to prepare them for college and a career in volcanology?
   c. What tools do volcanologists use?
   d. In what parts of the world do volcanologists do a lot of their work? (*Hint*: Research "Ring of Fire" in the Pacific Ocean.)

3. Create a Career Card using a large sheet of construction paper. Turn the paper horizontal on your desk and fold it into thirds. Title the card "Volcanologist."

4. On one third of the page, draw and color a picture of how you think a volcanologist would dress, including some of the tools that would be used. You can even draw a volcano in the background if you want to.
5. On the middle section, create a bulleted list of classes one might take in high school and college to become a volcanologist.
6. On the last section of the card, create a list of exotic places a volcanologist might travel in the world to do his or her work.

Marine Biologist: Lion Fish, Tiger Sharks, and Barracudas! Oh My!

Grade Levels: 3–4

Materials Needed:

- 1 large poster board
- Computer with Internet access

Steps:

1. Use the Internet to discover what marine biologists do. Take notes about what you find.
2. Answer the following questions as you read about marine biologists:
    a. What is the major field of study for marine biologists in college? What degree do they earn? Is earning a Bachelor of Science (BS) degree enough?
    b. What kinds of classes can students take in high school to prepare them for college and a career in marine biology?
    c. What kinds of jobs can marine biologists get? Create a list of at least 10 different marine biology jobs.
    d. Imagine you are a marine biologist. What would you study, and where would you live? Where would you work?

3. On a piece of poster board, design a social network profile of yourself as a marine biologist. Be sure to include a picture of yourself, where you work, what your major in college was, where you went to college, a short blog about an interesting marine animal, and a list of real Internet links to cool marine biologist information.
4. Ask your teacher to help you display your social network poster in the room.

Robotics Engineer:
Artificial Intelligence

Materials Needed:

- 1 large sheet of chart paper
- Computer with Internet access

Steps:

1. Use the Internet to discover what robotics engineers do. Take notes about what you find.
2. Answer the following questions as you read about robotics engineers:
   a. What is the major field of study for robotics engineers in college? What degree do they earn? Is earning a Bachelor of Science (BS) degree enough?
   b. What kinds of classes can students take in high school to prepare them for college and a career in robotics engineering?
   c. What kinds of jobs can robotics engineers get?
   d. What kinds of robots can robotics engineers design?
   e. What companies might hire a robotics engineer?

3. Imagine a large pizza company has hired you to automate the pizza-making process at their stores. Visit a local pizzeria and record the steps of pizza making that you see or find a video demonstrating the process on the Internet. Brainstorm different kinds of robotic devices that could replace human hands.
4. Use a large sheet of chart paper to draw your ideas for automation. Be sure to label all of the parts of your robotic inventions.
5. Ask your teacher to find a time for you to make a presentation about robotics engineers to the class. Be sure to share the information you found about robotics engineers as well as your pizza automation project.

Food Scientist: An Apple a Day

Grade Levels: 3–4

Materials Needed:

- 1 large sheet of chart paper
- Computer with Internet access

Steps:

1. Use the Internet to discover the different jobs food scientists do. Take notes about what you find.
2. Answer the following questions as you read about food scientists:
   a. What is the major field of study for food scientists in college? What degree do they earn? Is earning a Bachelor of Science (BS) degree enough?
   b. What kinds of classes can students take in high school to prepare them for college and a career in food science?
   c. What kinds of jobs can food scientists get?
   d. What companies might hire a food scientist?

3. Think of a food that you love that could be changed to make it better. For example, what if scientists could create ice cream that would not melt, yet would still be eaten frozen and still taste good? Or perhaps you enjoy the flavor of apples and watermelons and wish there were a way to create a new fruit called an "applemelon."
4. Use a large sheet of paper to design your new, improved food. Be sure to draw and color a picture of your food, and write a description of how the food will be created.
5. Ask your teacher to find a time for you to present your new food to the class.

Chapter 4

Planet Earth Projects

Earthquake Discovery

Grade Levels: 3–4

Materials Needed:

- Computer with Internet access

Steps:

1. Use your favorite Internet search engine and type in "U.S. Geological Survey Real-Time Earthquake Map" to see the most recent earthquakes that have occurred in the United States.
2. A map will pop up and you will be able to see all of the recorded earthquakes in the United States for the last week. Take some time to study the map. Are earthquakes occurring in your area? Have you felt them?
3. Scroll to the bottom of the page and find the menu titled "Learn" and click on "For Kids."
4. You will see a menu with 12 different topics to choose from. Take some time to read through the information in each of the topics.
5. Find one topic that interests you and do some extra research about the topic on other websites.
6. Compile all of the information you discover into a report, model, or demonstration to teach your class what you have learned.
7. Ask your teacher to find a time for you to present your work.

Volcanoes Making New Islands

Grade Levels: 3–4

Materials Needed:

- 1 large sheet of chart paper
- Art materials such as markers, crayons, and tempera paint
- Computer with Internet access

Steps:

1. Use your favorite Internet search engine to research "new volcanic islands." Take notes on the information you find. Look for articles that talk about the new island formed in December 2011 off the coast of Yemen, the new island near Tonga that emerged in 2009, and Surtsey, a volcanic island that surfaced off the coast of Iceland in 1963.
2. The Hawaiian Islands are a series of islands formed by volcanoes. Use your favorite Internet search engine and search "the formation of the Hawaiian Islands."
3. Take notes about what you discover about the Hawaiian Islands. Answer the following questions as you research:
   a. When you travel from the island of Hawaii and go northwest, why do the islands get older?
   b. What happened to the oldest islands in the Hawaiian chain? Where are they now?
   c. What part does erosion and weathering play in the life cycle of the Hawaiian island chain?

4. Create a wall mural of the Hawaiian island chain, including the older islands that are now submerged. Be sure to label each of the islands.
5. Write an essay to explain the life cycle of a volcanic island.
6. Ask your teacher to find a time for you to present your mural and essay with the class.

Comparing Landforms and Ocean Geography

Grade Levels: 3–4

Materials Needed:

- Computer with Internet access

Steps:

1. Use your favorite Internet search engine to research landforms. Create a chart that includes the name of each landform, a small sketch, a definition of the landform, and where you might find the landform in the United States (if applicable).

2. Now use your favorite Internet search engine to search "visual ocean floor." You will find several labeled pictures that show the topography of the ocean floor. Create a chart similar to the one you made in Step 1, listing the name of each ocean floor feature, a small sketch, and a definition of the feature.

3. Study the two charts you created. Are the landforms we can see so different from the ocean floor features we cannot see?

4. Create a Venn diagram comparing landforms to ocean floor features. How many are alike?

5. Ask your teacher to find a time for you to present your Venn diagram and charts to the class.

Natural Resources

Grade Levels: 3–4

Materials Needed:

- 1 copy of a blank United States map

Steps:

1. Use a natural resources map in your social studies book to identify at least six major natural resources in the United States.

2. Create a chart that lists each resource and include a list of products that are made using each resource. For example, one natural resource found in the United States is crude oil. Many products are made from crude oil such as tar, some rubber products, gasoline, kerosene, and more.

3. Of the natural resources you listed, which are renewable? Discover what people are doing to replenish these resources.

4. Of the natural resources you listed, which are nonrenewable? What are people doing to conserve these resources?

5. Ask your teacher for a copy of a blank United States map. Create a map key, identifying a different symbol for each of the six natural resources you chose.

6. Mark all of the places on the map where these natural resources are found in the United States. Color and title your map.

7. Write a report telling what you discovered about each of the resources, what products are made from them, and how they are being conserved or replenished.

8. Choose one natural resource from your list and write a persuasive paragraph to your class compelling them to conserve or help restore the natural resource.

9. Ask your teacher to find a time for you to share your chart, map, report, and paragraph with the class.

Chapter 5
Interdependence Projects

You Are the Boss

Grade Levels: 3–4

Materials Needed:

- 1 copy of A Questionnaire (p. 28)
- Video camera (optional)

Steps:

1. Imagine that you have just announced the opening of a new company. Because you are the boss and owner, a television reporter is on the way out to interview you.
2. Be prepared to answer the questions the reporter will ask. Use a copy of A Questionnaire to record your answers.
3. Ask a classmate to read the part of the reporter while you answer the questions. You can do this on videotape or live in front of the class (like a play).
4. Have students give you feedback about whether or not they would pay for your goods or services based on the interview you gave.

A Questionnaire

What business are you in?

What product or service does your business sell?

What made you decide to get into this business?

Do you expect to make a profit in the first year, or do you think it will take more time?

Does your product or service provide a need or want?

What three characteristics do you think are most important to the success of your business or any business?

What is the best reason you can give people to use your product or service?

What is the most important thing you want your customers to know about you as the owner of this business?

Interdependence

Grade Levels: 3–4

Materials Needed:

- Poster board
- Markers
- Dice
- Game board markers
- Computer with Internet access

Steps:

1. Research the term "interdependence" as it relates to United States products and goods that are imported and exported. Choose a specific country to research and discover what the country imports and exports. For example, what does Honduras export that the United States would import? What does the United States export that Honduras imports?
2. Create a game board that shows a ship sailing from a port in the United States to a port in a country that we trade with.
3. Write positive and negative events that happen along the way. For example, "Hurricane delays travel—lose one turn" or "Smooth seas—move ahead one space."
4. Make markers and use a die to tell you how many spaces to move. Create a set of rules for your game and also an explanation of how one wins the game.
5. Play the game with another classmate, so that if there are any problems with the game, you can redesign it before offering the game to the class.

The History of Money

Grade Levels: 3–4

Materials Needed:

- Computer with Internet access

Steps:

1. Use your favorite Internet search engine to research the history of money.
2. Write a reader's theater script or skit that explains the following:
   a. What was used before people decided to use coins and paper to pay for things?
   b. When did people start using coins?
   c. When did people start using paper money?
   d. When did people start using credit cards?
   e. Predict what will come next.

3. Ask your teacher to allow your classmates to help you practice and present the play.
4. Perform your play for an audience.

Money Around the World

|||||||||||||||||||||||||||||||||||||||||||||||||||||||||||||||||||||||||||||||||||||||||||||||||||||||||

Grade Levels: 3–4

Materials Needed:

- 1 copy of Currency Values Graphic Organizer (p. 32)
- Computer with Internet access

Steps:

1. Research the currencies (money) used in different parts of the world. For example, dollars are used in the United States, many countries in Europe use euros, and in Honduras, lempira are used.
2. Make a list of countries and the names of their currencies.
3. Use your favorite Internet search engine to find the conversion rate or value of the dollar in 10 foreign countries.
4. Use the Currency Values Graphic Organizer to compile your information.
5. Share your information with the class.

Currency Values Graphic Organizer

Directions: List the country, name of its currency, and the value of the country's currency compared to the American dollar below.

Country	Name of Currency	Value compared to $1.00	Is the U.S. dollar worth more or less than the currency in this country?
France	*euro*	*1 U.S. Dollar = 0.77 euros*	*less*

Chapter 6
Environment Projects

Population Migration

Grade Levels: 3–4

Materials Needed:

- None

Steps:

1. Consider what happens when a builder creates a new 50-acre housing development. People and pets are moving in, but what is moving out? As the population of humans increases, this scenario takes place all over the world and is probably taking place in your community now.

2. Think about the small critters that live around your area. How would they be displaced if a new housing development were built? Where would they go? Or would they stay? What would they eat? What would they drink? What problems might this cause?

3. Make a list of animals in your area that live in parks and other areas not populated with humans. This list may include animals the size of deer and coyotes, down to those the size of field mice and snakes. This list should contain at least 25 different animals.

4. Choose one animal from the list and imagine it could write to us and share its feelings with us. Write a letter from the point of view of the animal that explains the reasons why the animal would have to leave the area and the problems that might arise if the animal decided to stay. Be sure to end your letter with the decision the animal makes (if it decides to stay or leave).

5. Ask your teacher to find a time for you to share your letter with the class.

Food Chains

||||||||||||||||||||||||||||||||||||||||||||||||||||||||||||||||||||||||||||||||||||||||||||||||||||||||||||||||||||||||||||||||||

Grade Levels: 3–4

Materials Needed:

- 1 large sheet of construction paper
- Computer with Internet access

Steps:

1. Use your favorite Internet search engine to research food chains. Take notes about what you learn. Try to answer the following questions as you research:
   a. What is the most important part of the food chain and why?
   b. Define and list examples of producers, primary consumers, secondary consumers, tertiary consumers, and decomposers.
   c. What is always at the bottom of a food chain? Why are living things at the bottom of a food chain important?
   d. Define herbivores, carnivores, and omnivores.

2. Choose one ecosystem in your area to research. This could be a local lake or pond or even your own backyard. Visit the area and create a list of animals and insects you see.
3. Find the largest animal on your list. Discover what this animal eats. For example, you may have seen a rabbit. The rabbit eats grass. Grass is grown using energy from the sun.
4. Draw several food chains that could exist in the ecosystem you chose on a large sheet of construction paper. Be sure to label each food chain, categorizing each plant or animal as a producer, consumer, or decomposer.
5. Ask your teacher to find a time for you to present your work to the class.

Food Webs vs. Food Chains

||||||||||||||||||||||||||||||||||||||||||||||||||||||||||||||||||||||||||||||||||||||||||||||||||||

Grade Levels: 3–4

Materials Needed:

- 1 large sheet of chart paper
- Computer with Internet access

Steps:

1. Use your favorite Internet search engine to research the difference between a food chain and a food web. Take notes about what you learn and write a paragraph explaining the differences between the two.
2. Brainstorm and list at least 30 animals, insects, and plants that live in your area.
3. Use the Internet to help you discover what each animal, insect, or plant eats or needs to survive.
4. Imagine what would happen if one of the living things in your food web suddenly migrated or died. How would this affect the rest of the food web?
5. Choose one living thing from the food web that suddenly vanishes. Write a short play from the affected animals' point of view. The play should explain the problems the animals are facing as a result of one part of their food web disappearing as well as the solutions they create to solve the problem.
6. Gather a group of friends to help you practice your play.
7. Ask your teacher to find a time for you to present your play to the class.

Environmental Changes

Grade Levels: 3–4

Materials Needed:

- Computer with Internet access

Steps:

1. Choose one ecosystem in your area to research. This could be a local lake or pond or even your own backyard. Visit the area and create a list of animals and insects you see. Try to list at least 30 living things.

2. Imagine that this area was suddenly affected by a drought, wildfire, or a flood. What effect would this have on the plants and animals in the area?

3. Choose five animals or insects from the list. Write a news report script that tells about flood or drought. In your report script, include interviews with each of the animals or insects that explains how each has been affected and what its plans for the future entail. For example, if your backyard has suffered a drought and you are interviewing a grasshopper, the grasshopper might say,

> It certainly hasn't been a very "hoppy" summer. We've been trying to find green grass to eat, but more often we've been eating dry grass or the hard green leaves from the shrubs. If it doesn't rain soon, we'll have to hop to a pond or lake so we can survive.

4. Invite some of your friends to help you practice the script.

5. Ask your teacher to find a time for you to share your scripted news report with the class.

Food Webs

Grade Levels: 4–5

Materials Needed:

- 1 large sheet of chart paper
- Library access or computer with Internet access

Steps:

1. Visit the library or use your favorite Internet search engine to discover all of the components of a food web in a biome. Be sure to find the definitions and examples of the following parts of a food web: producer, primary consumer, secondary consumer, tertiary consumer, decomposer, predator, prey, herbivore, carnivore, scavenger, parasite.

2. Choose a biome to research. List many plants and animals that live in the biome. Label each animal with an appropriate word that describes where it is in the food web. For example, a coyote would be a tertiary consumer, a predator (mostly), a carnivore, and a scavenger.

3. Create a Glogster mash-up food web of photographs of each animal from your research. Be sure to include the labels for each animal. Don't forget to include the sun, as the sun is the source for all energy in a food web.

4. Ask your teacher to find a time for you to share your mash-up with the class.

Effects of Overpopulation

Grade Levels: 4–5

Materials Needed:

- None

Steps:

1. Think about what would happen in a food web if a consumer, such as a deer, suddenly became too numerous. Brainstorm a list of potential problems that could occur and the effect overpopulation would have on a particular area. Think about negative effects on the biome itself and also how the overpopulation might affect people.

2. Some states allow the hunting of deer each year. Often there are limits on the number of bucks (male deer) that can be shot, as well as limits on does (female deer) that can be killed. Imagine what might happen if the government suddenly outlawed deer hunting. Do you think this would cause an overpopulation problem, or do you think nature would solve the problem itself? Think about food becoming scarce in one area. What would the animals in that area do?

3. Create a list of things that man does to interfere with nature. Be sure to include things like building dams, highways, and neighborhoods in your list. How would these manmade items contribute to an overpopulation of deer in an area?

4. Write a story from the point of view of a yearling (a fawn that is more than a year old). It may be helpful to plan your story by developing a graphic organizer first. The yearling is old enough to understand the natural environment and knows when man comes that things will change. Choose one of the things in your list that man does to interfere with nature to include in your story. As the deer, be sure to explain how this one act causes an overpopulation of deer in the area where you live. Describe several problems you are having as a result of what man has done, and tell about your plans to survive.

5. Ask your teacher to find a time for you to share your story with the class.

Oxygen-Carbon Dioxide Cycle

|||||||||||||||||||||||||||||||||||||||||||||||||||||||||||||||||||||||||||||||||||||||||||||

Grade Levels: 4–5

Materials Needed:

- 1 large piece of chart paper
- Computer with Internet access

Steps:

1. Use your favorite Internet search engine to research the oxygen-carbon dioxide cycle. Be sure to answer the following questions as you research:
    a. What is photosynthesis?
    b. What living things use photosynthesis to produce food?
    c. What do these living things need to promote photosynthesis?
    d. What is produced as a waste product of photosynthesis?
    e. Where does the waste product go?
    f. What living things need the waste product of photosynthesis to survive?
    g. What is cellular respiration? What gas is used in cellular respiration?
    h. What is the waste product of cellular respiration?
    i. How is cellular respiration related to photosynthesis?
    j. How do living things get energy from cellular respiration?

2. Draw and label a picture of the oxygen-carbon dioxide cycle on a piece of chart paper. Choose at least two plants and two animals to include in your drawing.
3. Write a paragraph about how the oxygen-carbon dioxide cycle works on the chart, labeling the flow of carbon dioxide and oxygen between the plants and animals.
4. Ask your teacher to find a time for you to share your chart with the class.

One Animal's Survival

Grade Levels: 4–5

Materials Needed:

- Computer with Internet access

Steps:

1. Think about the way humans have slowly displaced animals in ecosystems as we have built homes, neighborhoods, communities, and entire cities.

2. Choose one animal that is native to your area and research the effects humans have had on the population of the animal. Try to answer the following questions as you research:
   a. Where did this animal live before your community was built?
   b. Where did this animal get its food and water?
   c. Where did this animal have its young?
   d. What has happened to this animal as a result of cutting down trees and clearing brush, building homes and roads, using ponds and lakes for recreation, and other human activities?
   e. Where do you see this animal now? What do you predict will happen to this animal in the future?

3. Write an essay telling what you learned about the animal you researched. Be sure to include the answers to all of the questions you addressed in your writing.

4. Ask your teacher to find a time for you to present your essay to the class.

Chapter 7
Myths Projects

Mythical Sayings

Materials Needed:

- Art paper
- Markers or paint
- Computer with Internet access

Steps:

1. Recognize that many old sayings in the English language have their roots in Greek and Roman mythology. Many of these sayings were inspired by famous characters from mythology and by persons and cultures that existed when the myths were created.
2. Select one of the following sayings (in italics) to research:
   a. I'm really good at writing; it's proofreading that is my *Achilles' heel.*
   b. The guard in front of the palace seems to have *stoic endurance.*
   c. You really don't want to go there and open a *Pandora's box.*
   d. I love our vacation home in the mountains even if it has *Spartan conditions.*

3. Write what the old saying means in words that you would use with a friend.
4. Create your own sentence using the old saying you selected, then draw an illustration that would artistically explain the reference.
5. Ask your teacher to help you find an appropriate place to display your finished product.

Time Travel

Grade Levels: 3–4

Materials Needed:

- 1 copy of Time Traveler Script (p. 43)

Steps:

1. Research life in ancient Rome and take notes about the way people dressed, ate, celebrated, relaxed, and made a living.
2. Use the information you have gathered to complete the rest of the Time Traveler Script that has been started for you.
3. Practice the finished script with another classmate.
4. Ask your teacher to find a time for you to present your play to the class.

Differentiated Projects for Gifted Students © Prufrock Press Inc.

Permission is granted to photocopy or reproduce this page for single classroom use only.

42

Time Traveler Script

Imagine you and a friend are traveling in a time machine. After doing research, finish writing the script below with at least three other events or activities you could have seen at this time on this day.

Settings on time machine:
- Date: 500 B.C.
- Place: Rome

Time Traveler 1: What is all that noise I hear?

Time Traveler 2: I'm not sure but it sounds like it is coming from up there in that stadium-like building.

TT1: I wonder if we arrived on a public holiday.

TT2: I think we have. They had lots of public holidays celebrating the Roman gods. I think that building is called the circus.

TT1: I love the circus. You mean they have elephants and clowns?

TT2: No, not that kind. The ancient Romans built open stadiums for gladiator fights and chariot races. They were long and narrow in an oval shape.

TT1: Let's get closer. That would be so cool to watch.

TT2: Not if you were a slave. That's who had to fight and die or drive those dangerous chariots.

TT1: What is so dangerous about the chariots?

TT2: You notice that they only have two wheels. What you can't tell is that they are very lightweight.

TT1: That doesn't make sense. The chariots are being pulled by four horses. It must be hard to keep the chariot under control.

TT2: That's the point. Just like cars and races today, there are bound to be accidents. Unfortunately, the chariot drivers were not all expected to survive, and they had no safety equipment.

TT1: So why did they risk their lives to do this?

TT2: Because if you survived and won several races you might earn enough money to buy your freedom.

TT1: Okay, let's see something else. All of a sudden chariot racing doesn't seem that cool after all.

TT2: If you want we could set the time machine for the day before or the day after so we can see what happens when the citizens aren't all gathered to celebrate a holiday.

Now complete the script, writing about three more places in Ancient Rome that you visit in your time machine.

E Pluribus Unum

Grade Levels: 3–4

Materials Needed:

- 1 copy of Mythical Character Argument (p. 45)

Steps:

1. Understand that although very few people speak Latin today, the language still exists and surrounds us.
2. Locate and examine coins and paper money to find the Latin phrase *E pluribus unum*. This means "out of many, one" and is included on most money in our country and is also written on the official seal of the United States.
3. Explain the meaning of *E pluribus unum*.
4. Read the Mythical Character Argument.
5. Define the italicized Latin sayings then rewrite the paragraph using words your classmates would understand.

Mythical Character Argument

I have heard complaints about Pluto *ad nauseam*. I have to do something about it. My brother, Neptune, owes me a favor. You know, *quid pro quo*. I will ask him to handle the situation for me. He can come visit me to discuss this or *vice versa*. I trust him. He is a *bona fide* friend and *semper fidelis*. The *status quo* in the underworld, where Pluto reigns, is completely unsatisfactory and out of control. I realize it is mostly *mea culpa* that I have let the problem go on for so long. I asked Pluto to improve the noise level, poor conditions, *et cetera*. Unfortunately I have seen no improvement. It is time to *carpe diem*. I have too much responsibility running Mount Olympus to leave at this moment. I will give Pluto one last chance before I descend from my throne and visit my rage upon him. For the time being, Neptune will carry out this favor. He will set things right.

The Elements of a Myth

Grade Levels: 3–4

Materials Needed:

- 1 copy of The Elements of a Myth sheet (p. 47)

Steps:

1. Understand that myths have the following common elements:
   a. mortals (humans) and immortals (beings that live forever);
   b. gods, goddesses, and heroes;
   c. characters with superhuman or magical powers;
   d. polytheism—the belief in more than one deity or god;
   e. explanations of the natural world, historical events, or lessons that teach a moral; and
   f. plots with real-world and imaginative settings.

2. Find a myth that has all of the elements listed above and tells of heroic deeds by a Greek or Roman god or goddess.
3. Read the myth, then fill in The Elements of a Myth sheet.
4. Write a summary of the myth you read.
5. Ask your teacher to find a time for you to share your summary and to teach the class about the elements of a myth.

The Elements of a Myth

Name of the myth you read:

_____

Names of mortals, immortals, gods, goddesses, and heroes in the story:

_____

_____

_____

Describe the heroic or brave characteristics the main character had.

_____

_____

_____

_____

_____

Describe the events this myth explained or the lesson you could learn from it.

_____

_____

_____

_____

What was the plot, and how did the myth end?

_____

_____

_____

_____

_____

Chapter 8

Organisms Projects

Earth Needs Plants!

Grade Levels: 3–4

Materials Needed:

- Library access or computer with Internet access

Steps:

1. Visit the library or use your favorite Internet search engine to research the importance of plants on Earth. Try to answer the following questions as you read:
    a. What do plants need in order to survive?
    b. What is photosynthesis? What gas do plants need for photosynthesis? What gas do plants expel?
    c. What is transpiration?
    d. How can transpiration and photosynthesis help humans?
    e. Do you think we could survive on Earth without plants? Why or why not?
    f. Why is pollination important?
    g. Why are plants called producers?

2. Using all of the information you gathered by answering the questions above, write a short report explaining the importance of plants on Earth.
3. Then, write a children's book and a song set to a familiar tune to teach younger students about the importance of plants.
4. Ask your teacher to find a time for you to share your book and song with a younger class.

Producers, Consumers, and Decomposers

Grade Levels: 3–4

Materials Needed:

- 1 large sheet of chart paper
- Computer with Internet access

Steps:

1. Choose one ecosystem in your area to research. This could be a local lake or pond or even your own backyard. Visit the area and create a list of plants, animals, and insects you see. Try to list at least 40 living things.

2. Use your favorite Internet search engine to define and learn about producers, consumers, and decomposers. Be sure to find information to define primary consumers, secondary consumers, and tertiary consumers. List examples of each of these groups.

3. Return to the list you created earlier. Using a large sheet of chart paper, classify each living thing you saw into one of the five groups: producers, one of the three kinds of consumers, or decomposers. After you finish categorizing, check to make sure each of the groups is represented. For example, if you discover that you did not list any decomposers, return to the ecosystem and look for earthworms, mushrooms, or other decomposers doing their job in the area. Try poking with a stick under rocks, piles of leaves, or in damp areas.

4. Add any missing information to your classification chart.

5. Write a paragraph about each of the five groups. Each paragraph should answer the following questions:
   a. What makes this group different from the others?
   b. What kinds of living things are in this group?
   c. How is this group dependent on others for survival?

6. Ask your teacher to find a time for you to present your classification chart and paragraphs to the class.

Life Cycles

Materials Needed:

- Two large sheets of chart paper
- Library access or computer with Internet access

Steps:

1. Visit the library or use your favorite Internet search engine to research the life cycles of one of each of the following kinds of animals: insect, reptile, and mammal.
2. Draw and label a picture of each life cycle on a large sheet of chart paper.
3. Create a three-way Venn diagram using three large, intersecting circles on another large sheet of chart paper. Write the name of each animal beside each of the circles. Record common attributes of all of the life cycles in the center where all of the circles intersect. Record common attributes between two animals where two circles intersect. Record the differences in areas where the circles are not intersecting.
4. After completing your comparisons, research the life cycles of the following: insect: aphid; reptile: Western diamondback rattlesnake; and mammal: duckbilled platypus. Take notes about the life cycle of each of these animals. How do these animals compare to the ones you originally chose?
5. Write a summary of what you discovered about animal life cycles.
6. Ask your teacher to find a time for you to present your charts, Venn diagram, and writing with the class.

Eating in the Ocean

Grade Levels: 3–4

Materials Needed:

- 1 large sheet of chart paper
- Library access or computer with Internet access

Steps:

1. Use your favorite Internet search engine or visit the library to discover the ways in which some ocean animals get their food. You will find that the structure of their bodies often determines how ocean animals feed themselves. Choose at least three ocean animals to compare. Be sure to choose at least one animal that has tentacles, one kind of jellyfish, and one ocean mammal. Suggestions include sea cucumbers, sea anemones, humpback whales, octopi, and squid.

2. Draw and label the body parts of each animal you chose on a large sheet of chart paper. Write a short paragraph describing how each animal takes in food below each labeled picture. Be sure to list some of the kinds of food each animal eats.

3. Answer the following question on a separate sheet of paper: Do you think the structure of a sea animal's body determines the kinds of food the animal eats? Explain your answer.

4. Ask your teacher to find a time for you to share your chart and writing.

Structure and Function of Feet

Grade Levels: 4–5

Materials Needed:

- 1 large sheet of chart paper
- Computer with Internet access

Steps:

1. Research the foot/hoof and leg structures of the following animals using your favorite Internet search engine:
   a. frogs
   b. alligators
   c. horses
   d. spiders

2. Draw and label detailed pictures of each creature's foot/hoof and leg. On a separate sheet of paper, write a paragraph telling how the structure of the foot/hoof and leg helps the animal move in its environment. Be sure to include information about the activities for which the foot/hoof and leg are used.

3. Create a chart on a large piece of chart paper. On the left side of the chart, list the name of each animal. Attach your detailed drawing of the foot/hoof and leg of each animal next to its name. Next to the drawing, attach the writing you did explaining the structure of the foot/hoof and leg and the function it serves in helping the animal to move freely in its environment.

4. Ask your teacher to find a time for you to present your project to the class.

Complete vs. Incomplete Metamorphosis

Grade Levels: 4–5

Materials Needed:

- 1 large sheet of chart paper
- Library access or computer with Internet access

Steps:

1. Visit the library or use your favorite Internet search engine to discover the similarities and differences between a complete and incomplete metamorphosis. List and draw the steps of each life cycle and list several creatures that experience each kind of life cycle.

2. Create three Venn diagrams on a large sheet of chart paper. On one Venn diagram, compare the complete and incomplete metamorphosis of insects. On the second Venn diagram, compare the life cycle of a human to the complete metamorphosis. On the third Venn diagram, compare the life cycle of a human to the incomplete metamorphosis.

3. On a separate sheet of paper, write a report sharing your observations about each life cycle and how they are alike and different.

4. Ask your teacher to find a time to share your Venn diagrams and report with the class.

The Tail's Tale

Grade Levels: 4–5

Materials Needed:

- Computer with Internet access

Steps:

1. Use your favorite Internet search engine to research bottlenose dolphins, sperm whales, and great white sharks. Try to answer the following questions as you read general information about each kind of animal:
   a. Is this animal a fish or a mammal? How do we know?
   b. How does this animal propel itself through the water?
   c. Where are the fins placed on this animal?
   d. What is the structure of the tail on this animal?

2. Locate a picture of the skeletal structure of each animal. Locate a picture of a human skeleton. Compare the human skeletal structure to the skeletons of the three animals. Which skeletons are most alike?

3. Consider the way in which humans propel themselves through water. To which animals are we most similar?

4. Create a three-way Venn diagram to compare the three animals. Use all of the information you gathered in your comparisons.

5. Think about the differences between the way a mammal propels itself through the water versus how a fish swims. Write a report explaining the reasons you think whales and dolphins move their tails in an up-and-down motion, and sharks and other fish move their tails in a side-to-side motion.

6. Ask your teacher to find a time for you to present your report to the class.

Prehensile Parts

Grade Levels: 4–5

Materials Needed:

- 1 large piece of construction paper
- Dictionary

Steps:

1. Understand that all animals have adapted to living in their environments. One adaptation that many animals share is prehensile body parts.

2. Use a dictionary to define the word "prehensile." Then brainstorm a list of animals that have a body part that contains this quality. Remember, there are prehensile tongues, tails, noses, lips, feet, and hands in the animal kingdom. If you have trouble, you can go to the Internet for help.

3. Choose a few of the animals you listed and find specific information about their prehensile body parts. What is the body part used for? This may explain why this adaptation occurred.

4. Think about humans in comparison to the animals you researched. Besides our hands, do we have any other prehensile body parts? Why do you think this is true?

5. Create a chart on a large piece of construction paper. List each animal you researched and its prehensile body part, then write a short paragraph telling why you think these body parts adapted to become prehensile.

6. Ask your teacher to find a time for you to share your chart with the class.

Chapter 9
Maps Projects

Cartography

Grade Levels: 3–4

Materials Needed:

- Index cards
- Dictionary

Steps:

1. Imagine you are learning to be a cartographer, a person who studies and makes maps.
2. Select your specialty. What types of maps would you most likely want to study and make? Your choices include climate, economic, physical, political, topographic, or thematic.
3. Define each type of map on an index card with the word on one side and the description on the other side.
4. Write a paragraph that explains which of the specialties you would select and give at least three reasons why.
5. Ask your teacher to use your cards in the next lesson about maps.

Pick Two

Materials Needed:

- Art paper
- Markers
- Computer with Internet access

Steps:

1. Create an outline map of your state.
2. Identify the differences between climate, economic, physical, and political maps.
3. Select two of the four types of maps to add to your outline.
4. Use your favorite Internet search engine to locate the most current data. Add the two types of data to your map.
5. Check for accuracy before coloring your map.
6. Add a compass rose and map key for any symbols you use.
7. Ask your teacher to display your map in the classroom.

Topographic Maps

Materials Needed:

- Art paper
- Markers or paint
- Dictionary
- Clay

Steps:

1. Define "topographic map" and understand its purpose. Topographic maps are one of the most difficult kinds of maps to create. Visit the library and observe some of the globes. Some globes actually have topographical features such as tactile mountain ranges, valleys, and other geographical features.
2. You will be creating a topographic map. You may select a state or region of your choice.
3. Add a compass rose and map key to the map you create.
4. Ask your teacher if you can explain to the class what this map tells people and who would find this type of map useful.

Just for You

‖‖

Grade Levels: 3–4

Materials Needed:

- Art paper
- Markers or map colors
- Computer with Internet access

Steps:

1. Decide on a thematic map you would like to make. Examples include a map showing the population change of Michigan from 1990–2010; a map showing the states with the highest unemployment rates; or a map showing or tracking the places in the U.S. where hurricanes have struck in the last 10 years.
2. Complete the research before starting the map using your favorite Internet search engine.
3. Use map colors or markers to draw your map. Be sure the title of your map explains the theme or purpose of your map.
4. Include a key for any symbols you plan to use.
5. Share the map with your class.

Chapter 10
Matter Projects

Properties of Matter

Grade Levels: 3–4

Materials Needed:

- A wooden block
- Water
- A small bowl
- A glass
- A pencil
- Cooking oil
- Balloon
- 2 large pieces of chart paper
- Computer with Internet access

Steps:

1. Use your favorite Internet search engine to define the following words: matter, states of matter, solid, liquid, gas. Record the definitions on a piece of paper.
2. Create a chart to classify the materials for this experiment into the three states of matter.
3. Think about the characteristics of a solid. List as many attributes of solids as you can in the solids column of your chart.
4. Pour water into the bowl. Pour the water from the bowl to the glass. What shape did the water assume when you poured it into the bowl? Into the glass? Empty the water from the glass. Repeat the experiment by pouring a small amount of cooking oil into the glass, and then into the bowl. What shape did the cooking oil take in the glass and then the bowl? List the special attributes of liquids on your chart.

5. Gases are all around us. Look at the glass on the table. Gases such as oxygen, carbon dioxide, and nitrogen are inside and around the glass. Inflate the balloon. You have filled the balloon with carbon dioxide and other gases you breathed out from your lungs. List the special attributes of gases in the gases column of your chart.

6. Create a three-way Venn diagram using three large, intersecting circles on another large sheet of chart paper. Write the name of each state of matter beside each of the circles. Record common attributes of all states of matter in the center where all of the circles intersect. Record common attributes between two states of matter where two circles intersect. Record the differences in areas where the circles are not intersecting.

7. Ask your teacher to check your chart for accuracy and to find a time for you to present your chart and experiments to the class.

Solid, Liquid, Gas

Materials Needed:

- Cold water
- Hot water
- Large bowl
- Drinking glass (not a plastic cup)
- Ice cubes
- Library access

Steps:

1. Visit the library to locate books to learn about the three main states of matter: solids, liquids, and gases. Water is a fun kind of matter because it can exist in all three states.
2. Submerge a drinking glass in a large bowl of hot water for 5 minutes. Remove the glass and dry. Fill the glass halfway with ice cubes. Observe for one minute. Record what you see on a sheet of paper.
3. Now, fill the glass with the ice and add cold water. Allow it to stand for 10 minutes. What do you see on the outside of the glass? Record what you see.
4. Write a paragraph explaining the three states of matter you observed in the experiment. Be sure to use the following words in your writing: condensation, water, heat, cold, moisture.
5. Ask your teacher to read your paragraph to check for accuracy. Make any necessary changes to make your information correct.
6. Have your teacher find a time for you to demonstrate the experiments and share your writing with the class.

Mixtures and Solutions

Grade Levels: 3–4

Materials Needed:

- Several jars with lids
- Small gravel
- Sand
- Dirt
- Sugar
- Salt
- Water
- Computer with Internet access

Steps:

1. Use your favorite Internet search engine to learn about mixtures. Mixtures can be found everywhere in nature. A mixture is the combination of two or more things that can be separated again. Examples of mixtures are saltwater and concrete. Saltwater is the combination of salt and water, but we can separate them again by boiling the water in a pan. The salt will remain in the bottom of the pan because a higher temperature is required to boil the salt.

2. Define solute, solvent, and system to help you understand solutions. A solution contains two or more things that, when mixed, are evenly distributed in the solution and cannot be separated. An example of a solution is sugar and water. When we add sugar to water, it completely dissolves. You cannot separate the sugar from the water once it is dissolved.

3. Using the jars and different "ingredients" provided, conduct your own experiments creating mixtures and solutions. Add dry ingredients first, then add water to each jar. Shake the jars to combine the ingredients.

4. Create a chart where you can record the different items you mixed with water in each jar.

5. Decide whether each combination is a mixture or a solution. Write a few sentences about the combinations in each jar, explaining why you believe each is a mixture or a solution.

6. Ask your teacher to find a time for you to share your experiments and findings.

Sink or Float

Materials Needed:

- One ball of clay
- Aluminum foil
- 1 large bowl
- Water
- Paper clips
- Computer with Internet access

Steps:

1. Fill the bowl halfway with water. Drop in the ball of clay. Observe and record whether the clay sinks or floats.
2. Tear off a small piece of foil and crumple it into a ball. Drop the foil ball into the water. Observe and record whether the foil sinks or floats.
3. Dry the clay ball. Pinch the clay ball into the shape of a boat or a canoe. Place the clay boat on top of the water. Observe and record whether the clay boat sinks or floats. (If the boat is made correctly, it should float.)
4. Tear off a sheet of foil and work to shape a boat from the foil. This may take several designs. You should be able to create a foil boat that floats.
5. Think about large cruise ships, oil barges, and cargo ships. These vessels weigh thousands of tons each, yet float across oceans every day to carry people and products from place to place.
6. Use your favorite Internet search engine and write the definitions of the following words on a sheet of paper: buoyancy, displacement, mass, matter, gravity, and density.
7. Write a summary of the sink and float experiments you completed. Use the six vocabulary words from the previous step in your summary to explain your findings.
8. Ask your teacher to find a time for you to share the experiments and your findings with the class.

Classifying Matter

Grade Levels: 4–5

Materials Needed:

- Items to observe for physical properties such as a block of wood, a marble, different kinds of rocks, water, a spoon, or a penny.
- 1 copy of Classifying Matter (p. 67)
- A magnet
- A balance scale
- A bowl for water

Steps:

1. Scientists classify matter in many ways. They study physical properties of matter such as mass, magnetism, the physical state (whether it's a solid, liquid, or gas), the density (does it sink or float), and the solubility (does it dissolve in water).
2. Gather several of the items listed in the Materials section and a copy of the Classifying Matter sheet.
3. Conduct experiments on each kind of matter, filling in the Classifying Matter chart with your results.
4. Group your items by common physical properties and record the items in a list. For example, create a list of all of the magnetic items you tested. What characteristics do these items have in common (besides being magnetic)? List the characteristics of each group you create. Create a group and characteristics list of each physical property on the chart (except mass).
5. Think about the conclusions you can draw about each group you created. Make generalizations about each group. For example, "Iron nails are magnetic, so iron must be magnetic." Do research to see if your generalizations are correct or incorrect.
6. Ask your teacher to find a time for you to share your findings with the class.

Classifying Matter

Directions: Record each item you test in the column on the left. Measure the mass of each object using a balance scale. Fill in the appropriate information about each object as you test its physical properties.

Item	Mass	Magnetic?	Solid?	Liquid?	Gas?	Sink?	Float?	Solubility?

A Liquid Solid

Materials Needed:

- Equal amounts of cornstarch and water
- Magnet
- Balance scale
- Bowl of water
- 3 small cups
- Vinegar
- Dishwashing liquid
- Vegetable oil

Steps:

1. Mix equal amounts of cornstarch and water in a bowl.
2. Experiment with the mixture in the bowl. Answer the following:
   a. Is it a liquid or a solid?
   b. Does it have mass?
   c. Is it magnetic?
   d. If you add the mixture to water, does it sink, float, or dissolve?
   e. Is it a conductor or insulator?
   f. What happens when you pour the mixture out of the bowl and onto a table? Can you get the mixture back into the bowl? Can you form the mixture into a ball?

3. Make a T-chart on a separate sheet of paper. Brainstorm the properties of liquids and solids. For example, solids maintain their shapes, while liquids conform to the shape of the container in which they are placed.
4. Separate small amounts of the cornstarch and water mixture into several cups. Try adding a few drops of each of the following liquids to the mixture in each cup: vinegar, dishwashing liquid, and vegetable oil. Does adding the liquids have an effect on the mixture? Is it more or less like a liquid or solid?
5. Write a persuasive paragraph to share your thoughts on whether the cornstarch and water mixture is a liquid or solid or both. Be sure to use information from your T-chart in your paragraph.
6. Write a paragraph explaining what happened when you added vinegar, dishwashing liquid, and vegetable oil to the mixtures. Did adding any of these liquids make the mixture behave any more like a solid or liquid?
7. Ask your teacher to find a time for you to present your findings to the class.

Mixtures and Solutions

||||||||||||||||||||||||||||||||||||||||||||||||||||||||||||||||||||||||||||||||||||||||||||||||||||||||||||||||||||||||||

Grade Levels: 4–5

Materials Needed:

- Vegetable oil
- 4 different colors of food coloring
- Clear bowl
- Small cup
- Water
- Dropper
- Measuring spoons
- 1 copy of Mixtures and Solutions (p. 70)
- Computer with Internet access

Steps:

1. Use your favorite Internet search engine to define mixtures and solutions. Record the definitions on the Mixtures and Solutions sheet.
2. Complete the experiments on the Mixtures and Solutions sheet.
3. Ask your teacher to find a time for you to present your experiment to the class.

Mixtures and Solutions

A mixture is _____

_____

A solution is _____

_____

1. Fill a clear bowl ⅔ full of water.
2. Measure 1 tablespoon of vegetable oil into a small cup.
3. Drop 1–3 drops of each color of food coloring into the cup with oil. Draw and label a picture of what you notice below. Is this a mixture or a solution?
4. Mix the food coloring and oil until the food coloring drops are tiny. Pour the oil and food coloring into the bowl of water. Let the water sit for one minute. Draw and label a picture of what happened below. Is the water and food coloring a mixture or a solution? What happened to the oil?
5. Pour out the water, oil, and food coloring in a sink (be sure to rinse out the sink well). Add fresh water to the bowl. Add another tablespoon of oil to the cup. Carefully add 2–3 drops of each color of food coloring to the oil. DO NOT MIX!
6. Carefully pour the oil and food coloring into the bowl by slowly pouring the mixture down the inside of the bowl. Most of the food coloring should still be in blobs in the oil and not mixed into the water.
7. Use a sharpened pencil to poke the blobs of food coloring. What happens as you poke each blob of color?

How Strong Are Magnets

Grade Levels: 4–5

Materials Needed:

- 1 bar magnet
- 1 horseshoe magnet
- 1 ring magnet
- Paper clips
- 1 copy of How Strong Are Magnets? (p. 72)

Steps:

1. Measure the strength of each magnet by using nonmagnetic items through which the magnetic properties should pass. For example, place a magnet on the bottom side of a piece of paper, then place a paper clip on the top side. Can you still move the paper clip using the magnet?
2. Create a chart listing the different nonmagnetic items you used on one side and the types of magnets you used on the other side.
3. Experiment with nonmagnetic items of different thicknesses. Some items you may want to try include file folders, paperback books, textbooks, a chair, or even your table. Test the strength of each magnet and record the results in the table on the How Strong Are Magnets? sheet.
4. Ask your teacher to find a time for you to share the experiment and your findings with the class.

How Strong Are Magnets?

Directions: Place a check in the appropriate box when a magnet was strong enough to move a paper clip through the object.

	paper						
Bar Magnet	✓						
Horseshoe Magnet	✓						
Ring Magnet	✓						

Chapter 11

History and Tall Tales Projects

Real or Fiction?

Grade Levels: 3–4

Materials Needed:

- Library access
- Computer with Internet access

Steps:

1. Understand that tall tales are part of American history. These exaggerated stories usually involve settling the United States and sometimes center on characters who once existed.
2. Visit the library and select three tall tales to read. Record the main ideas from three tall tales based on three different characters.
3. Using your favorite Internet search engine, research the main character in each story.
4. Identify which, if any, of the characters were based on a real person.
5. Write a paragraph about each of the three tall tale characters you researched. The paragraph should include how they are unique, what they are famous for, and whether they are based on a real person or are purely fictional.
6. After reading the tall tales, create a list of elements that are present in most tall tales. For example, tall tales usually have a central character who performs extraordinary things. Often we do not know the origins of the character.
7. Ask your teacher to find a time for you to present your report to the class.

Tall Tale City Planning

Materials Needed:

- None

Steps:

1. Recognize that one common element of a tall tale is that the main character often disappears at the end of the story.
2. Imagine that there is a place where all tall tale characters reappear to live out their days. This place is called the "Tall Tale Character Frontier Town."
3. Brainstorm a list of living spaces that tall tale characters would need in order to make them all comfortable and happy. For example, you would need a place large enough for Paul Bunyan's blue ox.
4. List the types of buildings, stores, entertainment facilities, and services that would be necessary for the tall tale characters.
5. Explain the purpose for each building on your list. Be sure to include which tall tale character or characters this building was designed for.
6. Draw and label a rough draft of what the façade or face of the building would look like.
7. Ask your teacher to find a time for you to present your tall tale town to the class.

Tall Tale Regions

|||||||||||||||||||||||||||||||||||||||||||||||||||||||||||||||||||||||||||||||||||||||||||||||||||||||||||||||||

Grade Levels: 3–4

Materials Needed:

- 1 copy of Tall Tale Character Interview (p. 76)
- Computer with Internet access

Steps:

1. Understand that many tall tale characters and stories are set in specific states or locations.
2. Use your favorite Internet search engine to research where tall tale characters are said to have lived or worked. It could be a state or a region.
3. Select one tall tale character. Write a paragraph explaining why you think a particular tall tale character fits well with the history and location of that area.
4. Write a scripted interview for the tall tale character. Use the Tall Tale Character Interview sheet on page 76 to get started.
5. Ask a classmate to be either the character or the talk show host, and present the scripted show to your class.

Tall Tale Character Interview

Directions: Write a scripted interview for the tall tale character you've selected, using the script below to get you started.

Talk Show Host: Good afternoon, ladies and gentlemen. We have an exciting guest today who we will bring out in just a minute. Are you wondering who it is? I'll give you a hint. The character we will interview today is well-known in this area.

Tall Tale Character: Hello, I'm so happy to be here. This is the first talk show I've ever been invited to. I must say I am honored but a little nervous.

Talk Show Host: No, it is our honor. Please don't be nervous. Can you tell our audience your name and what you are known for?

Tall Tale Character:

A New Character

Grade Levels: 3–4

Materials Needed:

- Library access
- Art materials such as markers, crayons, map pencils, and blank paper

Steps:

1. Visit the library to choose and read several different tall tales.
2. Create a new tall tale character for the state or region in which you live.
3. Write a paragraph explaining why you think your particular tall tale character would fit well with the history and location of your area.
4. Write and illustrate a short tall tale featuring your new character in a story that explains what he or she does that is unique. Remember to include all of the elements of a tall tale in your story.
5. Present the tall tale to your classmates.

Chapter 12

Force, Motion, and Energy Projects

Gravity and Mass

Grade Levels: 3–4

Materials Needed:

- A balance scale
- Several unbreakable objects that can be weighed and dropped on the floor
- 1 copy of Gravity and Mass Recording Sheet (p. 80)
- Library access or computer with Internet access

Steps:

1. Use your favorite Internet search engine or visit the library to find information about Galileo. Specifically look for what Galileo discovered about gravity.
2. Think about dropping a bowling ball and a pin from the same height. Which object do you think will hit the floor first?
3. Conduct the experiment on the Gravity and Mass Recording Sheet.
4. Ask your teacher to find a time for you to share your research with the class.

Gravity and Mass Recording Sheet

Directions:

1. Write the name of each object being tested in the left column.
2. Weigh each object using the balance and record the mass in the middle column.
3. Select two items and drop them at the same time from the same height. Did they hit the ground at the same time or different times? Record the results in the right column, listing the two items and whether or not they hit the ground at the same time.
4. Repeat the experiment using all of the objects. Does mass affect the rate at which gravity pulls objects to Earth?

Object	Mass	What Happened?

Friction

Materials Needed:

- Library access or computer with Internet access

Steps:

1. Visit the library or use your favorite Internet search engine to find information about friction. Try to answer the following questions as you conduct your research:
   a. What is the force called friction?
   b. What does friction do?
   c. Why is friction important?
   d. What is the definition of work?
   e. How is friction related to work?
   f. What are some examples of friction?
   g. How are gravity and friction related?
   h. What are some ways people try to reduce friction to make work easier?

2. Imagine we lived in a world with little to no friction. This is what it might be like if we lived on the moon. Because the moon has much less gravity compared to Earth, there is also less friction.

3. Choose an outdoor game you like to play such as four square, soccer, or basketball. Brainstorm the difficulties of playing this game without friction or gravity. Would you be able to run? What would happen if you jumped or fell? What effect would almost zero friction and gravity have on the ball?

4. Write and illustrate a story about you and your friends trying to play this game in an area with nearly zero friction and gravity.

5. Ask your teacher to find a time for you to share your story with the class.

Heat Energy: Conductors

Grade Levels: 3–4

Materials Needed:

- 1 copy each of Heat Experiment 1 and Heat Experiment 2 (pp. 83–84)
- Aluminum foil
- Small square of carpet (unless the classroom is carpeted)
- 1 frozen tennis ball
- 1 room temperature tennis ball
- 1 meter stick
- 1 ice cube
- 10 inches of thin wire
- Computer with Internet access

Steps:

1. Use your favorite Internet search engine to research how heat travels. You will discover that heat travels through conduction, convection, and radiation. Locate the definitions of these words, and record the definitions and examples of each.
2. Conduct the experiments on the Heat Experiment sheets to understand how heat travels through conduction.
3. Choose one other way that heat travels (either convection or radiation) and research experiments you can complete that demonstrate how that form of heat transfer works. Gather the materials needed and conduct the new experiment.
4. Design a station for students to visit to learn about the ways heat travels. Use the experiment you found, as well as one of the experiments that was provided.
5. Ask your teacher to find a time for students to visit your station to conduct the experiments.

Heat Experiment 1:
Conductors and Insulators

Materials Needed:

- Aluminum foil
- Carpet

Steps:

1. Place a sheet of foil on a tile or wood floor and allow it to remain undisturbed for 10 minutes.
2. Remove your shoes and socks.
3. After 10 minutes, stand, placing one foot on the foil and the other foot on the carpet. Note the difference in temperature.
4. Talk with a classmate and describe the difference in temperatures between the foot on the carpet and the foot on the foil.
5. A good conductor of heat energy allows heat to move from a warmer object to a cooler object. A poor conductor of heat energy is called an insulator. Insulators block heat loss. A good example is a Styrofoam coffee cup. Of the carpet and foil used in this experiment, which was the insulator and which was the conductor?
6. Look around the classroom. Using what you've learned, create a list of conductors and insulators.

Heat Experiment 2:
Why Is Tennis a Summer Game?

Materials Needed

- 1 tennis ball at room temperature
- 1 frozen tennis ball
- 1 meter stick

Steps

1. Hold a meter stick and place the room temperature tennis ball at the top edge. Drop the ball and measure the height of the first bounce. Repeat this step several times to get a good average measurement of the bounce.
2. Repeat Step 1 using the frozen tennis ball.
3. Which ball bounced highest? Why do you think this happened?
4. The inside of a tennis ball is hollow, so we know that it is filled with gas molecules like nitrogen and oxygen. When balls bounce, they hit the floor and are slightly squashed, then spring back to their normal shape and travel in the opposite direction from which they came. When an object is heated, the molecules inside the object move faster. When an object is cooled, the molecules inside it move more slowly. The molecules in the room temperature tennis ball were moving at a normal rate, so the ball squashed and returned to its normal shape quickly and bounced as high as was expected. The molecules inside the frozen tennis ball were moving more slowly, meaning the ball squashed more slowly, returned to its normal shape more slowly, and did not bounce as high as the warmer ball.
5. The tennis ball acted as an insulator in this case. It was insulating the gas molecules inside the ball. When the gas molecules were warmer, the ball bounced higher. When the gas molecules were cold, the ball bounced lower.
6. Think about how this information would affect when people decide to play tennis. Do you think this experiment could be applied to other kinds of balls? As an optional activity, try the experiment with ping-pong balls, baseballs, volleyballs, soccer balls, or basketballs. Does cooling the gas molecules affect the ways the other balls bounce?

Newton's Laws

||||||||||||||||||||||||||||||||||||||||||||||||||||||||||||||||||||||||||||||||||||||||||||||||||||||||||||||||

Grade Levels: 3–4

Materials Needed:

- Computer with Internet access

Steps:

1. Use your favorite Internet search engine to search "Newton's 3 Laws of Motion." Click on the website with the title "Newton's 3 Laws of Motion."
2. Read through the information about Sir Isaac Newton. Then click to learn about each of the laws of motion. Take notes about each law of motion.
3. Take the quiz at the end to see what you learned. Go back to review any laws of motion that were unclear.
4. Click on the experiments to see different ways you can teach others about the laws of motion. If you choose, gather the supplies to perform both experiments.
5. Think about each of the laws of motion. How could you teach this information to your class?
6. Devise a way to teach and demonstrate Newton's Laws of Motion to your class. You can create a Prezi presentation, a video of yourself explaining each law of motion, or another project of your choice. Then create one or two experiments for students to perform that demonstrate one or all of the laws of motion.
7. Gather all of the materials necessary to complete your experiments and ask your teacher to find a time for you to present your information to the class.

Potential vs. Kinetic Energy

Grade Levels: 4–5

Materials Needed:

- Computer with Internet access

Steps:

1. Use your favorite Internet search engine to research the difference between potential and kinetic energy. Record the definition of each word, as well as several examples of each kind of energy.
2. Sketch drawings of potential and kinetic energy on a piece of paper. For example, a bicycle and rider sitting on top of a hill shows potential energy. The same bicycle and rider going down the hill shows kinetic energy. Potential energy is stored energy. Kinetic energy is the energy of motion.
3. Create a memory game with 10 pairs of cards. Brainstorm 10 examples where potential and kinetic energy can be seen. Draw a picture of potential energy on one card, and the kinetic energy of the same scene on another card to create the matches.
4. Play the game by matching the potential to the kinetic energy in each scene. Invite a friend to play the game with you.
5. Ask your teacher to set a time for you to teach potential and kinetic energy to the class. You might suggest using the game you created in a station for others to play.

Manipulating Energy

Grade Levels: 4–5

Materials Needed:

- 1 small toy car
- Triple beam balance
- A long piece of wood or a slanted table to use as a ramp
- Several small, dense objects to use as weights on the car
- Tape
- Chair
- A measuring tape or meter stick
- 1 copy of Manipulating Energy (p. 88)

Steps:

1. Build a ramp using a chair and a long piece of wood or a slanted table.
2. Place a car at the top of the ramp. At the top of the ramp, the car has potential or stored energy.
3. Release the car and measure the distance the car traveled beyond the ramp using a measuring tape or meter stick. When you release the car, it has kinetic energy or the energy of motion. Repeat this step two more times and calculate the average of the distances. Record the distance on the Manipulating Energy sheet.
4. Measure the tallest part of the ramp and record it on the Manipulating Energy sheet.
5. Measure the mass of the car using the triple beam balance and record it on the Manipulating Energy sheet.
6. You can manipulate the potential and kinetic energy of the car by changing its mass and changing the height from which the car is released.
7. Experiment with raising and lowering the height of the ramp and releasing the car. Record your results.
8. Move the ramp back to the original height. Experiment with adding mass to the car by securing small, dense items to the car with tape. Be sure to record the mass of the car plus the object for each experiment.
9. Which experiment caused the car to have greater potential and kinetic energy—raising the ramp height or adding mass to the car?
10. Ask your teacher to find a time for you to present your experiment to the class. Have the class make predictions about what will happen with the potential and kinetic energy of the car before you demonstrate each experiment.

Manipulating Energy

Baseline Trial

Item Being Tested	Mass of Item	Height of Ramp	Distance Traveled
Car			
Car			
Car			
Average Distance Traveled			

Raising the Ramp Trial

Item Being Tested	Mass of Item	Height of Ramp	Distance Traveled
Average Distance Traveled			

Adding Mass Trial

Item Being Tested	Mass of Item + Added Mass	Height of Ramp	Distance Traveled
Average Distance Traveled			

Manipulating Energy Graphs

Grade Levels: 4–5

Materials Needed:

- Equipment and results from the Manipulating Energy experiment
- Computer with Internet access

Steps:

1. Conduct the Manipulating Energy experiment if you have not already done so.
2. Create two graphs that demonstrate what happens to kinetic energy as you manipulate the height of a ramp or manipulate the mass of an object. Line graphs would be the best kind of graphs to display these results. Use your favorite Internet search engine to help you create the two line graphs.
3. Repeat the experiment, this time raising the ramp to the highest point in the original experiment and adding the greatest amount of mass. Repeat the experiment several times and record the results each time.
4. Graph the results of this final experiment using a line graph.
5. Think about the following question: Do you think there would ever be a time when adding too much height to the ramp or too much mass to the object in this experiment would cause negative results? Write a paragraph explaining your answer.
6. Ask your teacher to find a time for you to present your results to the class.

Potential and Kinetic Energy at the Amusement Park

Grade Levels: 4–5

Materials Needed:

- Computer with Internet access

Steps:

1. Think about your favorite amusement park. What is it about the attractions that keep you going back? Is it the big drops of the roller coasters? The feeling of flying on the swings? The slow motion of the Ferris wheel? The anticipation of waiting for the ride to start?

2. Create a list of five rides you have been on or would like to ride on someday. Each of these rides has potential and kinetic energy.

3. Use the Internet to find pictures of these rides or draw pictures of your own. You may only be able to draw the ride as it looks in the very beginning like the car going up the hill of a roller coaster.

4. Label each picture with places where there is potential energy or kinetic energy being used. Remember, as a roller coaster is being lifted to its highest point in the ride, it is storing potential energy. When it reaches the peak of the first big drop, the roller coaster is converting the potential energy to kinetic energy as it slips over the top. When the roller coaster reaches the bottom of the big drop and begins moving back up the tracks, it is using both kinetic energy of motion and is storing potential energy to keep it moving.

5. Create a PowerPoint presentation showing each ride and the labels of where the ride stores potential energy or creates kinetic energy. Be sure to tell the name of each ride and the park where the ride is found.

6. Ask your teacher to find a time for you to share your PowerPoint presentation with the class.

Chapter 13

Government Officials Projects

Local Government

Grade Levels: 3–4

Materials Needed:

- Computer with Internet access

Steps:

1. Understand that local governments get their power from state constitutions and how it is handled varies from state to state.
2. Use your favorite Internet search engine to research the local government where you live. You can use your local Chamber of Commerce office as a resource, as well. List the top local government official and the names of all of the people who serve under this official. Create a graphic organizer to complete this step.
3. List the job titles, names of the actual people with these titles, and how each of these people get their jobs. Are all of the positions at the local level elected by the people or are some appointed?
4. Identify an issue that is coming up at the next local government meeting or at a future meeting.
5. Research both sides of the issue, then write a persuasive letter to send to local officials expressing how you feel about the issue or matter coming before the council.

State Government

|||||||||||||||||||||||||||||||||||||||||||||||||||||||||||||||||||||||||||||||||||||||||||||||||||||||||||||||||||||||||||||||||||||||

Grade Levels: 3–4

Materials Needed:

- Computer with Internet access

Steps:

1. Understand that state governments get their power from the federal government from the U.S. Constitution and all states govern the same way.
2. Using your favorite Internet search engine, research your state government. List the top official (usually the governor) and the names of all of the people who serve under the governor. Create a graphic organizer to complete this step.
3. List the job titles of the people who serve below the governor, names of the actual people with these titles, and list how each of these people get their jobs. Are all of the positions at the state level elected by the people or are some appointed?
4. Identify an issue or vote that is coming up at the next legislative session.
5. Research both sides of the issue, then write a persuasive letter to send to the governor expressing how you feel about the issue coming before the legislative branch of your state government.

National Government

Materials Needed:

- Computer with Internet access

Steps:

1. Understand that the national or federal government gets its power from the U. S. Constitution.
2. Using your favorite Internet search engine, research the structure of the U.S. government. List the top official (the President of the United States) and the names of all of the people who serve under the President. Use a graphic organizer to complete this step.
3. List the job titles of the people who serve in the federal government below the President of the United States, the names of the actual people with these titles, and how each of these people get their jobs. Are all of the positions at the national level elected by the people or are some appointed? Create a color key on your graphic organizer that distinguishes between elected and appointed officials.
4. Identify an issue or vote that is coming up at the next legislative session.
5. Research both sides of the issue, then write a persuasive letter to send to the President of the United States or your state representative in Washington, DC, expressing how you feel about the issue.

Vote for Me

Grade Levels: 3–4

Materials Needed:

- Computer with Internet access
- Poster board or chart paper
- Markers

Steps:

1. Imagine that one day you will run for a public government office.
2. Decide whether you would prefer local, state, or federal government.
3. Identify which job you would want most and explain in a paragraph what the job would involve. What exactly would you be doing?
4. Add an additional paragraph explaining why you think you would be especially good at this job.
5. Use your favorite Internet search engine to research campaign posters. Design a campaign poster for yourself for this job. You can create the poster by hand using poster board or electronically using a website like Glogster.
6. Ask your teacher for a time when you could share your essay and campaign poster with the class.

Local Government

Grade Levels: 4–5

Materials Needed:

- Computer with Internet access

Steps:

1. Understand that local governments get their power from state constitutions and how it is handled varies from state to state.

2. Use your favorite Internet search engine to research the local government where you live. The local Chamber of Commerce would also be a good source of this information. List the top official and the names of all the people that serve under this official. Create a graphic organizer to complete this step.

3. List the job titles, names of the actual people with these titles, and list how each of these people get their jobs. Are all of the positions at the local level elected by the people or are some appointed? Use a color key to designate which jobs are elected and which are appointed.

4. Identify an issue that is coming up at the next local government meeting or future meeting.

5. Research both sides of the issue then write a persuasive letter to send to local officials expressing how you feel about the issue or matter coming before the council. Call or e-mail one of the local officials to get their opinion on how they feel and will vote on this issue.

6. Write a follow-up letter to the local official with whom you communicated thanking the person for his or her time.

7. Share your original letter and any correspondence you received regarding your letter with your class.

8. Attend or watch the next local meeting where the issue you are concerned about will be discussed and write a short summary of the meeting and the resolution of the issue. Share the summary with your class.

State Government

Grade Levels: 4–5

Materials Needed:

- Computer with Internet access

Steps:

1. Understand that state governments get their power from the federal government from the U.S. Constitution and all states govern the same way.

2. Use your favorite Internet search engine to research your state government. List the top official, governor, and the names of all the people that serve under the governor. Create a graphic organizer to complete this step.

3. List the job titles of the people who serve below the governor, names of the actual people with these titles, and how each of these people get their jobs. Are all of the positions at the state level elected by the people or are some appointed? Use a color key to designate which jobs are elected and which are appointed.

4. Identify an issue or vote that is coming up at the next Legislative session.

5. Research both sides of the issue then write a persuasive letter to send to the governor expressing how you feel about the issue coming before the legislative branch of state government. Call or e-mail the governor's office to find out how he or she plans to vote on the issue you selected.

6. Write a follow-up letter expressing your pleasure or displeasure with his or her stand on the issue you selected. Be sure to provide at least three or four statements that support your opinion on the issue.

7. Share the issue and information you discovered and encourage your classmates to send a letter expressing their views on the issue that you shared.

8. Follow the progress of the issue through your state government website and the news.

National Government

Materials Needed:

- Computer with Internet access

Steps:

1. Understand that the national or federal government gets power from the U.S. Constitution.
2. Use your favorite Internet search engine to research the structure of the U.S. Government. List the top official, the President of the United States, and the names of all of the people who serve under the President. Use a graphic organizer to complete this step.
3. List the job titles, names of the actual people with these titles and list how each of these people get their jobs. Are all of the positions at the national level elected by the people or are some appointed? Use a color key to designate which jobs are elected and which are appointed.
4. Identify an issue or vote that is coming up at the next legislative session.
5. Research both sides of the issue then send an e-mail to the President of the United States or one of your state representatives, asking how they will vote on this issue. Then write a persuasive e-mail to send to the President of the United States or your state representative in Washington, DC, expressing how you feel about the issue.
6. Write a follow-up e-mail to the person who responded to your inquiry thanking the person for his or her time.
7. Share your original letter and any correspondence you received regarding the issue with your class.
8. Monitor the news and/or your state representative's website for progress on the issue you are following.

Vote for Me

Materials Needed:

- Computer with Internet access
- Poster board or chart paper
- Markers

Steps:

1. Imagine that one day you will run for a public government office.
2. Decide whether you would prefer local, state, or federal government.
3. Identify which job you would want most and explain in a paragraph what the job would involve. What exactly would you be doing?
4. Add an additional paragraph explaining why you think you would be especially good at this job.
5. Use your favorite Internet search engine to research campaign posters that have been successful for historical figures in the past. Write a paragraph that explains how campaign posters have changed over time. Design a campaign poster for yourself for this job using a style you found in your research. This poster may be done by hand or using a computer program with design capabilities.
6. Ask your teacher for a time when you could share your essay and campaign poster with the class.

Chapter 14

Electric Energy Projects

Static Cling

Grade Levels: 3–4

Materials Needed:

- Water balloons (not inflated or filled with water)
- 1 large balloon
- 1 piece of wool
- 1 cup of rice cereal
- Water faucet
- 1 copy each of Static Electricity Experiment 1, Static Electricity Experiment 2, and Static Electricity Experiment 3 (pp. 101–103)
- Computer with Internet access

Steps:

1. Use your favorite Internet search engine to research static electricity. As you research, try to answer the following questions:
   a. What is an atom? What are the parts of an atom?
   b. Draw a model of an atom on a piece of paper.
   c. Define protons, electrons, and neutrons. What kind of electrical charge does each part of an atom have?
   d. What special property do electrons have that protons and neutrons don't share?
   e. If an item is an insulator (does not conduct heat or electricity), are its electrons held together tightly or loosely? How tightly are elec-

trons bound in a conductor (an item that conducts heat or electricity easily)?

    f. How does the phrase "opposites attract" relate to static electricity?

2. Use the Static Electricity Experiment sheets to help you learn more about static electricity.

3. Ask your teacher to find a time for you to present what you have learned to the class.

Static Electricity Experiment 1: Opposites Attract

Materials Needed:

- Water balloons (not inflated or filled with water)
- 1 large balloon
- 1 piece of wool

Steps:

1. Inflate two water balloons and tie.
2. Rub the balloons on your hair or on a piece of wool for at least one minute.
3. Place the balloons gently against the wall. As long as your wall is not stone or cement, the balloons should stick. If you have trouble getting the balloons to stick, try sticking them to the back of a plastic chair.
4. Why do you think the balloons stuck to the wall?
5. Take the piece of wool and rub it on the wall in one spot for one minute. At the same time, rub a large, inflated balloon on your head. After one minute, try to stick the balloon to the place on the wall where you rubbed the wool. What happens?
6. In the first part of the experiment, the electrons in the wall and the electrons in the balloons had opposite charges. When you create an opposite electrical charge between two objects, the objects will be attracted to one another. In the second part of the experiment, you created two charges that were alike by rubbing the wall and balloons. When two charges are alike, objects repel one another.

Static Electricity Experiment 2: Jumping Cereal

Materials Needed

- 1 large balloon
- 1 piece of wool
- 1 cup of rice cereal

Steps

1. Pour a few pieces of rice cereal on the table.
2. Rub a balloon on your head or on a piece of wool for at least 1 minute.
3. Hover the balloon over the rice cereal on the table and observe what happens.
4. How is this experiment similar to Experiment 1? Can you use the same principles to explain what happened?

Static Electricity Experiment 3: Bending Water

Materials Needed

- 1 large balloon
- 1 piece of wool
- Water faucet

Steps

1. Inflate a large balloon and tie.
2. Go to a large sink. Rub the balloon on a piece of wool for at least one minute.
3. Turn on the sink. Slowly move the charged part of the balloon toward the stream of water. Observe the shape of the stream of water.
4. In this case, the balloon repels the water. The balloon and running water have the same charge, so the electrons in the balloon and the electrons in the running water repel one another, causing the water to bend.

Electromagnets

Materials Needed:

- 3-inch iron nail
- 5-inch iron nail
- Strong bar magnet
- 2 D-size batteries
- 24 inches of insulated copper wire
- Wire strippers
- Duct tape
- Paper clips
- 1 copy of Electromagnet Experiments (p. 105)
- Computer with Internet access

Steps:

1. Use your favorite Internet search engine to research electromagnets. You will discover that electromagnets are very powerful magnets that are created using electricity and are used to pick up very heavy objects.
2. Conduct the experiments on the Electromagnet Experiments sheet.
3. Create a demonstration of the strength of an electromagnet compared to a bar magnet.
4. Ask your teacher to find a time for you to show your demonstration to the class.

Electromagnet Experiments

Materials Needed:

- 3-inch iron nail
- 5-inch iron nail
- 2 D-size batteries
- 24 inches of insulated copper wire
- Wire strippers
- Duct tape
- Paper clips
- Other batteries of different sizes (optional)

Steps:

1. Have a teacher help you use the wire strippers to remove about 1 inch of insulation from each end of a 12-inch piece of copper wire.
2. Carefully coil the wire around the middle of the 3-inch nail. Leave about 7 inches of the wire hanging off of each end of the coil.
3. Stack two D-size batteries on top of one another, with the positive side of one battery touching the negative side of the other. Tape the batteries together where they meet.
4. Tape one end of the wire to the top of the battery stack. Tape the other end of the wire to the bottom of the battery stack. This makes an electromagnet.
5. Determine the number of batteries the 3-inch nail electromagnet will pick up and record the number.
6. Repeat the experiment with the 5-inch nail.
7. Optional: You may repeat the experiment using different-sized batteries and alternating the different sizes of nails. Which combination of batteries and nails creates the strongest electromagnet?

Producing Electricity

Materials Needed:

- Library access or computer with Internet access

Steps:

1. Visit the library and your favorite Internet search engine to research how we produce the electricity that we use. You will discover that a lot of our electricity is produced by coal plants, nuclear power plants, wind farms, hydroelectric plants, solar panels, and more.

2. Choose one way the United States produces electricity to research. As you read, try to answer the following questions:
   a. How is electricity produced using this source?
   b. Where does the electricity go once it is made?
   c. What are the pros for producing electricity this way?
   d. What are the cons for producing electricity this way?

3. Brainstorm a creative way to present your information. Be sure to use some kind of visuals as you put your presentation together.

4. Ask your teacher to find a time for you to present your information to the class.

Imagine a Day . . .

Materials Needed:

- None

Steps:

1. Imagine a world where electricity had never been discovered and harnessed. This world actually existed more than 100 years ago. Your great- and great-great-grandparents likely lived in a world where people were not as dependent on electricity as we are today.

2. Think about all of the items that would not exist if it weren't for the existence of usable electricity. Could you live a day without electricity? It is doubtful you could live an entirely electricity-free day without packing a tent and venturing into the wilderness.

3. Get several sheets of paper. Starting when you first wake up, create a list of everything you use that requires electricity. Don't forget to list things like the refrigerator, because it keeps your milk cold.

4. Keep adding to the list for an entire day. Challenge your friends to create the same list. Compare your lists—it's likely you forgot to consider some items.

5. Ask your teacher to find a time for you to host a discussion with your class about our dependence on electricity. Some possible questions to promote discussion are:
   a. Do you think you could live an entire day without electricity?
   b. Do you think the world is a better place because of the discovery and harnessing of electricity?

Create a Light Switch

Grade Levels: 4–5

Materials Needed:

- A 9-volt battery
- 1 set of holiday lights (cut apart so that each light has two wires coming from it—have an adult help you use a wire stripper to expose the wires coming from each bulb)
- 5 inches of insulated copper wire with wire exposed on each end
- 1 paper clip
- 1 index card
- 2 metal brads
- Duct tape
- 1 copy of Light Switch (p. 109)

Steps:

1. Follow the instructions on the Light Switch sheet to create your own light switch.
2. Brainstorm ways you could use the light switch you created to make a flashlight. Try to answer the following questions as you brainstorm:
   a. How could you make the light more reflective and therefore brighter?
   b. What could you use for the casing of the flashlight?
   c. How would you attach the switch? You may need to take the components of the switch off of the index card to create your flashlight.

3. Experiment with different designs and build your flashlight.
4. Write a detailed list of materials and instructions so that others can repeat your steps.
5. Ask your teacher to find a time for others to follow the instructions you created to build their own flashlights.

Light Switch

Materials Needed

- A 9-volt battery
- 1 set of holiday lights (cut apart so that each light has two wires coming from it)
- 5 inches of insulated copper wire with wire exposed on each end
- 1 paper clip
- 1 index card
- 2 metal brads
- Duct tape

Steps

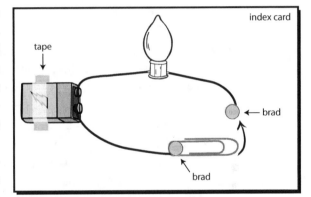

1. Secure a 9-volt battery to a large index card using tape. Twist one end of a stripped holiday light wire (have an adult help you expose the wire) around one of the terminals of the battery. Secure with duct tape.
2. Cut another piece of insulated copper wire and strip one inch of the insulation from both ends (have an adult help you). Secure one end of the wire to the other battery terminal with duct tape.
3. Poke one brad through the paper clip and index card like shown in the picture above. Secure the loose end of the copper wire to the brad. Poke the other brad through the index card so that it is close enough to be touched by the paper clip *and* touch the other holiday light wire.
4. Attach the other end of the holiday light wire to the second brad and secure with duct tape.
5. Move the paper clip to touch the second brad. If you built your switch correctly, the bulb will light. If the bulb does not light, examine all of the wire connections to be sure the circuit is complete.

Natural Batteries

Materials Needed:

- 1 lemon
- Other assorted fruits and vegetables
- Materials for student-chosen experiment
- 1 set of holiday lights
- Computer with Internet access

Steps:

1. Use your favorite Internet search engine to find an experiment for building a lemon battery. The Zoom website (http://pbskids.org/zoom) has some fun fruit battery experiments. Gather the supplies necessary to build the battery and complete the experiment. Repeat using other fruits of your choice.

2. Test each battery you create by determining the number of lights it will light in a string of holiday lights. You will have to cut the set of lights apart—try cutting the wires between every three bulbs. Have an adult help you strip the insulation of the wires at either end so you can twist and connect the lights back together by twisting the wires at the end of each strand during the experiment. Will the fruit or vegetable light a strand of three lights? Six lights? Nine lights? More?

3. Which fruit or vegetable makes the strongest battery? Write an essay describing the experiments you completed with each fruit or vegetable, telling which made the strongest battery and how you knew.

4. Ask your teacher to find a time for you to demonstrate the different natural batteries you made and to present your findings.

Electric Vocabulary

Materials Needed:

- Dictionary or computer with Internet access

Steps:

1. Use a dictionary or your favorite online dictionary to record the definitions of the following electricity-related words:
   a. conductor
   b. insulator
   c. electricity
   d. static electricity
   e. circuit
   f. complete circuit
   g. incomplete circuit
   h. switch
   i. battery
   j. electron

2. Create a fun way to teach the vocabulary and definitions to a friend. You could make electronic flashcards using a computer, regular flashcards using index cards, modify an existing game by using the flashcards as questions instead of the ones that came with the game, or create your own unique vocabulary lesson.

3. Ask your teacher to find time for you to present your lesson to the class or to small groups of students.

Let There Be Light!

Materials Needed:

- A variety of batteries (5 round watch batteries, 2 AA batteries, 2 AAA batteries, 2 C batteries, 2 D batteries, 2 9-volt batteries)
- 1 set of holiday lights (cut apart so that each light has two wires coming from it—have an adult help you use a wire stripper to expose the wires coming from each bulb)
- Paper
- Markers
- Duct tape

Steps:

1. Experiment with lighting the bulbs by placing one end of a holiday light wire to the positive side of a battery and the other end to the negative side of the same battery. Can you get a bulb to light with each of the batteries?
2. Twist two lights together to form a chain. Repeat Step 1 using two lights. Were you able to get both lights to light using each kind of battery?
3. Repeat the experiment with three lights twisted together.
4. Use duct tape to tape all like-sized batteries together. Repeat the experiment using the batteries taped together. Keep adding more lights to the chain until the batteries will not light them.
5. Create a bar graph and graph the batteries by the amount of power each had.
6. Using what you have learned about the strength of different kinds of batteries from experiments and observations, write an essay explaining why you think some electronic devices need smaller/larger batteries than others.

Chapter 15
Cultures Projects

One Big Family

Grade Levels: 3–4

Materials Needed:

- Computer and Internet access
- Poster board
- Markers
- 1 copy of Foods and Celebrations (p. 114)

Steps:

1. Use your favorite Internet search engine to research the various groups of immigrants that have settled in your state.
2. Make a list of the countries they came from on the Foods and Celebrations sheet.
3. Research these countries and see what foods and celebrations have been integrated into your state's customs. Record them on the Foods and Celebrations sheet.
4. Create a poster that illustrates your findings.
5. Ask your teacher to help you find time to present your poster to the class.

Foods and Celebrations

Directions: Use the information you found in your research to fill in the boxes for each country.

State: _____

Country	Foods	Celebrations

Birthday Celebrations Around the World

Materials Needed:

- Computer with Internet access

Steps:

1. Understand that every child in the world has a date of birth, but not every child celebrates a birthday or celebrates his or her birthday the way you do.
2. Write a paragraph that explains the way you celebrate your birthday.
3. Select three other countries from three different continents and use your favorite Internet search engine to research the way children in that culture celebrate the day of their birth. Create a graphic organizer to keep track of what you discover.
4. Take at least one idea from each of the three countries you researched and write a paragraph showing how you could incorporate these ideas into your next birthday celebration.
5. Share what you found with your parents and classmates.

Getting to Know You

Grade Levels: 3–4

Materials Needed:

- Computer with Internet access

Steps:

1. Use your favorite Internet search engine to research an immigrant who had a big influence on your city, county, or state. Try to answer the following questions as you read:
   a. Where was this person born?
   b. What was his or her life like in the native country?
   c. Why did this person leave his or her native country?
   d. What was this person hoping to find?
   e. What is this person best known for?
   f. What do you think this person would think of how his or her influence has affected the city, county, or state?

2. Imagine you could bring this person back for a personal interview on a talk show.
3. Write the script between the interviewer and the guest.
4. Ask a classmate to be either the interviewer or guest. Practice the script.
5. Ask your teacher to find a time for you to present your script to the class.

Introducing . . .

Materials Needed:

- Computer with Internet access

Steps:

1. Use your favorite Internet search engine to research well-known authors, artists, or poets who have made names for themselves in your state.
2. Select one person about whom you would like to learn more. Create a list of questions you would like to answer as you research.
3. Choose a way to introduce this person to your classmates. You could create a PowerPoint presentation featuring some of an artist's work, a recording of a musician's music, or create an illustrated collection of a poet's poetry. Be creative in the way you choose to present the information.
4. Put together your presentation and ask your teacher to find a time for you to share it with your classmates.

Multicultural Dinner

Grade Levels: 4–5

Materials Needed:

- 1 copy of Multicultural Dinner (p. 119)
- Computer with Internet access

Steps:

1. Imagine that you live in a very diverse neighborhood and school. You embrace the differences and enjoy learning about new customs and traditions, especially when it involves food. Your family has invited the newest neighbors over for dinner. You have been asked to help create a menu that will work for the dietary restrictions of your guests. Use your favorite Internet search engine to find appropriate foods to serve your three guests who follow Islamic, Hindu, and Kosher diets.

2. Take notes about each diet's traditional foods and foods that are taboo. Use the Multicultural Dinner sheet for your notes.

3. Plan and write a menu that will satisfy the dietary needs of your three guests for this dinner party. (Note: Don't prepare three separate meals.) Try to develop a combination of foods that will appeal to all three guests.

4. Draw and color a detailed bird's-eye view of the table with all of the foods you plan to serve.

5. Ask the teacher to help you find an appropriate time to present or display your menu and picture.

Multicultural Dinner

Directions: Take notes below as you read about each special diet. Find and record the information in each row.

	Islamic	Hindu	Kosher
Traditional Foods			
Taboo Foods			

Multicultural Restaurant

Grade Levels: 4–5

Materials Needed:

- Computer with Internet access

Steps:

1. Your class has decided to open a temporary restaurant in your school cafeteria for a weekend fundraiser. You want to attract a lot of people so you want to offer a unique menu. You have narrowed down your choices to a Paleolithic diet, Inuit diet, or a Mediterranean diet. Use your favorite Internet search engine to research these three diets.
2. Make a chart that lists popular foods for each of these three diets that you think your peers will eat.
3. Decide which of the three diets you will use as your guide.
4. Create a menu that will utilize the foods from that diet. Leave room under each entrée for a description.
5. Describe the food using lots of sensory language that will make each item hard to resist.
6. Decide on a name for your restaurant that reflects the type of food you serve. Write the name of your restaurant on the menu.
7. Decorate the menu to go along with the restaurant name, theme, and type of food.
8. Ask the teacher to help you find an appropriate time to present or display your work.

Diversity Can Be Tasty

Materials Needed:

- 1 copy of Diversity Can Be Tasty (p. 122)
- Computer with Internet access

Steps:

1. Imagine that during lunch, you notice the new students at your table have foods you don't usually eat or even recognize. When you ask what kinds of diets they follow, you learn that one of your new friends is vegan, one is a fruitarian, and one is on a macrobiotic diet. You don't want to feel uninformed, so you decide to research these diets using your favorite Internet search engine. Use the chart on the Diversity Can Be Tasty sheet to organize your notes.
2. Research a flexitarian diet, and take notes to complete the flexitarian column on the Diversity Can Be Tasty sheet.
3. Assume that you follow the flexitarian diet. Understand how your friends' diets are alike and different from your diet.
4. Analyze the similarities and differences between the flexitarian diet and the other three diets. Determine how the flexitarian diet is similar and different to each of the three other diets.
5. Write a multiparagraph essay, with each paragraph describing how the flexitarian diet is similar and different when compared to each of the other diets.
6. Create a final copy of your essay.
7. Ask your teacher to help you find an appropriate time to present your information.

Diversity Can Be Tasty

Directions: Research all four kinds of diets and list how each diet approaches the food groups in the chart below.

	Vegan	Fruitarian	Macrobiotic	Flexitarian
Protein				
Fruits				
Vegetables				
Dairy Products				
Fats/Other				
Grains				

New Restaurant in Town

Grade Levels: 4–5

Materials Needed:

- Computer with Internet access

Steps:

1. Suppose that your cousin's family has decided to open a restaurant, and they want to serve food that represents a specific ethnicity. They want your help to decide what kind of restaurant they will open. First, define "ethnic food."
2. Use your favorite Internet search engine to research what kinds of ethnic restaurants have the highest rates of success in the United States.
3. Research the different types of ethnic restaurants that already exist in your town.
4. Use your research results to make a recommendation to your cousin's family. Write a short report telling which ethnic restaurant you think will be most successful for them and support your recommendation with facts.
5. Brainstorm a creative name for the ethnic restaurant that you suggested. It should attract positive attention and help people understand the kind of food the restaurant will serve.
6. Write a jingle that includes the name of the restaurant and some of the foods that will be on the menu.
7. Record a song that could be used as an advertisement on a radio station. Most radio spots are about 30 seconds. Use sound effects or musical instruments to enhance the jingle.
8. Ask the teacher to help you find an appropriate time to present your work.

Chapter 16

Create a New State Projects

State Anthem

Grade Levels: 3–4

Materials Needed:

- Computer with Internet access

Steps:

1. Understand that most states have a state song or anthem. Some states have more than one.
2. Imagine you have established a new state and need an anthem or song. Use your favorite Internet search engine to discover anthems from several states. List the details that you liked most in those songs. For example, the state song of Oklahoma lists physical characteristics of the state that make it unique.
3. Make a list of the important things you want to include in your anthem. These might include the name of your state, the beauty or uniqueness of your land, the dramatic history of the founding of your state, the type of government and/or resources you have, and so on. It will be a song that will be sung at all important public events.
4. Write an anthem for your new state. Be sure to include the things you brainstormed and researched in the previous step. You can choose to use the background music of one of the state songs you researched or even use the music from your own state song, as it is a familiar tune.
5. Ask your teacher to help you find an appropriate time for you to sing your new state song to the class.

Raise the Flag

Materials Needed:

- Large piece of construction paper
- Markers or paint
- Computer with Internet access

Steps:

1. Understand that all states have a flag with colors and symbols that make a statement about their state.
2. Use your favorite Internet search engine to discover your state flag, its colors, and the symbolism of the colors and pictures used. Research the U.S. flag and the symbolism of the stars, stripes, and colors.
3. Again using your favorite Internet search engine, search "state flags." Select and draw five state flags and research the symbolism used in the designs of the flags.
4. Decide what you want your flag to say about your state. List the symbols you want included. Write a paragraph explaining the symbols you chose.
5. Decide what colors you will use in your flag and write a paragraph telling what the colors symbolize.
6. Draw or paint your flag on a large piece of construction paper.
7. Ask your teacher to help you find an appropriate place to display your flag and writing.

Happy Holiday

Materials Needed:

- Poster board
- Markers

Steps:

1. Understand that some states have holidays that are celebrated just in that state. It might be the date when the state became a part of the United States. It might be a date when something unique happened in that state or the birthday of a person who was an important part of the history of that state. It could also be a festival that celebrates something that state is known for, like a product that is exported to other states or countries.
2. Brainstorm a list of possible holidays for your newly created state.
3. Decide when the holiday will be celebrated, why the holiday will be celebrated, and how the holiday will be celebrated.
4. Create a poster that incorporates all of this information so people who live in your new state will know what to do and when to do it.
5. Ask your teacher to help you find an appropriate place to display your poster.

State Bird

Grade Levels: 3–4

Materials Needed:

- Computer with Internet access

Steps:

1. Understand that all states have a state bird. The state bird may have been chosen because it is the bird with the largest population in the state or it could have been chosen for other reasons.
2. Use your favorite Internet search engine to find the list of state birds for the 50 states in the United States.
3. Brainstorm a list of possible birds for your newly created state.
4. Research birds and their characteristics to decide what would make a bird worthy of being named the state bird of your newly created state.
5. Create a presentation of your choice or a written report that identifies your state bird and explains why this bird was selected for this honor.
6. Ask your teacher for a time to present your information to the class.

Chapter 17
Adaptations Projects

Comparing Bird Beaks

Grade Levels: 3–4

Materials Needed:

- 1 copy of Bird Beak Shapes (p. 130)
- Library access or books about birds

Steps:

1. Visit the library and find several books about different kinds of birds.
2. Skim each book, looking specifically for information about what the bird eats and how it uses its beak and talons to obtain food. Fill in the Bird Beak Shapes sheet as you complete your research.
3. On the Bird Beak Shapes sheet, sketch each kind of bird beak.
4. Write a paragraph about each kind of bird. Each paragraph should contain the following information:
   a. where the bird lives
   b. what the bird eats
   c. how the shape of the bird's beak helps it function as a tool for the bird
5. Ask your teacher to find a time for you to share the information you collected about birds with the class.

Bird Beak Shapes

Directions: Fill in information you discover about each kind of bird beak in the chart below. Draw the beak shapes in the space provided.

Bird	What Does It Eat?	Sketch of Its Beak

Differentiated Projects for Gifted Students © Prufrock Press Inc.
Permission is granted to photocopy or reproduce this page for single classroom use only.

Comparing Root Systems

|||||||||||||||||||||||||||||||||||||||||||||||||||||||||||||||||||||||||||||||||||||||||||||||||||||||||||||||||||||||||||||||||||||||||||||||||

Grade Levels: 3–4

Materials Needed:

- 1 copy of Root Chart (p. 132)
- Computer with Internet access

Steps:

1. Understand that plants have many different types of root systems that each serve different purposes. Some of the most common types of root systems are taproot, adventitious root, and fibrous root systems.
2. Use your favorite Internet search engine to research each kind of root system. Fill in the Root Chart.
3. On a separate sheet of paper, draw and label each type of root system. Create a pros and cons list for each type of root system. For example, plants with taproot systems can get water from deeper sources during drought, but it makes them more difficult to pick (in the case of carrots or dandelions).
4. Think about different biomes on Earth and the kinds of plants that grow there. Choose one kind of biome and research plant adaptations in that biome. For example, many plants in desert regions have grown root systems that go all the way to a ground water source.
5. Choose one plant from the biome and draw and color a picture of the plant above ground and the root system below the ground.
6. Write a paragraph about the biome in which the plant lives and how it has adapted to survive.
7. Ask your teacher to find a time for you to present the information you gathered.

Root Chart

Directions: Fill in the information about root systems on the chart below.

Root System	Description of Root System	Plants With This Root System

Comparing Leaves

||||||||||||||||||||||||||||||||||||||||||||||||||||||||||||||||||||||||||||||||||||||||||||||||||||||||||||

Grade Levels: 3–4

Materials Needed:

- A variety of leaves
- Crayons
- Computer with Internet access

Steps:

1. Gather a variety of leaves (at least eight) from trees and plants near your school or home. Identify the name of each plant you took a leaf from if you can. Also track the area from which you took the leaf. Was it a flowerbed, garden, field, pond, or other area?

2. Cut several sheets of copy paper in half. Place one leaf under a sheet of paper and use a crayon to gently color over the leaf so that you can see its shape and veins. Be sure to add the name of the plant and the area where you found it if you have that information.

3. Repeat the last step for the remaining leaves you found.

4. Describe the color and texture of each leaf on each sheet of paper. Is the leaf waxy, rough, or pokey? Is it bright green, dull green, or another color? Does the leaf have more than one color?

5. Use your favorite Internet search engine or books from the library to learn more about leaves and how their shapes and textures affect the survival of the plant. For example, many trees in the rainforest have leaves that have a flat, round shape with a pointed tip. These leaves are called "drip tip leaves." Their function is to move water quickly away from the other leaves to prevent mold growing on them in the wet environment. On trees with needle leaves like pine trees, the needles work to hold more water because they are usually found in a drier climate. And cactus pads (which are actually its leaves) are thick so they can hold a lot of water.

6. Try to add more information about leaf shapes and textures to the information you already gathered.

7. Ask your teacher to find a time for you to present your leaf project to the class.

Comparing Animals in Biomes

Grade Levels: 3–4

Materials Needed:

- 1 large sheet of chart paper
- Library access
- Computer with Internet access

Steps:

1. Visit the library and locate books about the desert and tropical rainforest. Look for books that have sections that talk about the animals that live in the desert or rainforest.
2. Make a chart on a large sheet of chart paper that shows the different kinds of animals that live in the rainforest and the desert.
3. Now, use your favorite Internet search engine to research several animals from each biome. Try to find information about how the animals have adapted to live in that particular biome.
4. Write a story about an animal from the rainforest that suddenly had to move to the desert or vice versa. In the story, animals that live in the biome already should share their ideas about how the new animal can adapt to the environment. For example, if the animal moved from the rainforest to the desert, one way to adapt would be to hunt at night and sleep during the day. The animal might also learn to eat cactus as a way to get water.
5. Ask your teacher to find a time for you to share your chart and story with the class.

Chapter 18

U.S. History Projects

Which George, by George?

Grade Levels: 3–4

Materials Needed:

- 1 copy of Which George? (p. 136)

Steps:

1. Recognize that two very famous men lived during the same time and were both named George:
   a. George Washington, who was the Commander-in-Chief of the Continental Army and the first President of the United States of America.
   b. King George III, who was the King of England and the rest of the British Empire including the American colonies.

2. Read the facts on the Which George? sheet. Use your favorite Internet search engine to determine the facts that match each George.
3. Create a similar quiz using facts you discovered about each George.
4. Ask your teacher to set a time for your classmates to take the quiz you created to see how close they come to the correct answers without research.

Which George?

Directions: Read each statement. Write either GW for George Washington or K for King George III in the blank provided.

_____ Which George was sometimes considered a traitor?

_____ Quote from Samuel Johnson: "Of him we are much inclined to hope great things." (Samuel Johnson was the greatest English writer of his day.)

_____ The following quote by "Light-Horse Harry" Lee was talking about which George: "first in war, first in peace, and first in the hearts of his countrymen."

_____ This George had 2 children.

_____ This George had 15 children.

_____ He hired German troops to help fight for his side.

_____ He accepted help from French leaders.

_____ This George was married to a German princess.

_____ He refused to be King of America.

_____ This George was the last King of America.

_____ This George encouraged his soldiers to ambush, use quick speed, travel lightly, and blend in to the scenery.

_____ He taught his soldiers that the honorable way to fight is to march openly into battle in columns and rows, shoulder to shoulder.

_____ At one time during the war he wrote, "I am wearied almost to death. I think the game is pretty near up."

_____ He had a House of Lords and House of Commons to make decisions for the people.

_____ At one time during the war he said, "I think I shall soon hear . . . loyal subjects, returning to that duty they owe to an indulgent sovereign."

Changing Times

Grade Levels: 3–4

Materials Needed:

- ▪ Computer with Internet access

Steps:

1. Understand that many things have changed over time but one thing has not: Ever since the citizens of the United States elected their first President, they have wanted to know what the President is thinking, planning, and concerned about.

2. Use your favorite Internet search engine to research how forms of communication between the President and his constituents, or fellow Americans, have changed over time.

3. Write a reader's theater or play that explains these changes. Include at least three former Presidents (such as Calvin Coolidge, Franklin Roosevelt, and Harry Truman) and the current president in your reader's theater.

4. Conclude your play with a prediction about the way future presidents will communicate with American citizens.

5. Ask classmates to volunteer to read various parts in your play.

6. Ask your teacher to find a time for you to present your play to the class.

Communication

Grade Levels: 3–4

Materials Needed:

- Computer with Internet access
- 1 large sheet of chart paper

Steps:

1. Use your favorite Internet search engine to research the progress of communication beginning in 1900 to today.
2. Create a timeline on a large sheet of chart paper that shows the development of different inventions and innovations. Be sure to include dates and illustrations.
3. Predict what you think might be the next communication device that might be developed by the year 2050. Draw a picture of this new device on your timeline.
4. Ask your teacher to help you find an appropriate time to present your work.

One of the Greats

Grade Levels: 3–4

Materials Needed:

- Dictionary
- Computer with Internet access

Steps:

1. Recognize that one of the most popular and well-known people from American history is Benjamin Franklin. Many people mistakenly think he was one of our Presidents. Franklin was a statesman, diplomat, inventor, postmaster, musician, scientist, printer, and a very well-respected author.
2. Use a dictionary or the Internet to help you define the literary term "adage." One of Franklin's better known adages is "There has never been a good war or a bad peace."
3. Use your favorite Internet search engine to research, then list, 10 of Franklin's most popular adages.
4. Clarify what you think Franklin meant by each adage and comment on whether or not you think it could still be true today.
5. Present the adages and your thoughts in a presentation style of your choosing. Include one piece of clip art, a photo, or an illustration and your comments for each adage.
6. Ask your teacher to select an appropriate time for you to present your presentation.

Chapter 19

Conducting Investigations Projects

Safety Matters

Grade Levels: 4–5

Materials Needed:

- Two poster boards
- Markers
- Computer with Internet access

Steps:

1. Use your favorite Internet search engine to compile a list of common safety rules for conducting experiments in a science lab. Try to find and record at least 20 different rules. Be sure to have your teacher look at your list of rules because there may be others that should be added.
2. Use a computer to create a list of rules for science experiments in your classroom. Use a font large enough to create a two-page document.
3. Draw a picture that includes several scenes within a science lab on both posters. These scenes would include tables, chairs, science equipment, and so on. Do not color the posters at this time. One poster is going to show people conducting safe experiments following all of the rules. The other poster is going to show people breaking many of the rules while conducting experiments.

4. Begin drawing in people demonstrating the correct ways to conduct science experiments on one poster. For example, in this poster, the people will be wearing safety goggles, girls will have their hair in ponytails, and everyone will be wearing shoes.

5. Illustrate the same people not following safety rules on the other poster. These people might be eating and drinking in the lab, playing with the equipment, running around, pouring chemicals in a trash can, and so on.

6. Ask your teacher to find a time for you to present your safety rules and posters to the class. You can use the posters as teaching visuals by having students identify the safe behaviors going on in one poster and the dangerous behaviors happening in the other. Your teacher may even wish to display your posters and rules in the classroom.

Steps to Investigation

Materials Needed:

- Materials for the experiment you choose
- Library access or computer with Internet access

Steps:

1. Visit the library or use your favorite Internet search engine to research the steps to the scientific method. Write each step with a brief description of each on a sheet of paper. Draw a flow chart that shows the order of the steps from beginning to end.

2. Define the following words as you conduct your research: cause and effect, hypothesis, independent variable, dependent variable, analysis, and conclusion.

3. Visit the library to find a book about science fair projects. Skim the pages of a book to find a research idea that appeals to you. Brainstorm a list of questions you might ask as a result of reading this experiment. For example, if the experiment was about how roots always grow down, your question could be, "Is there a way to make roots grow another direction besides down?"

4. Choose one of the questions you created as the basis for an investigation using the scientific method. Ask your teacher to approve your experiment idea. Follow the steps of the scientific method to conduct your experiment, write about the findings, and report the results.

5. Ask your teacher to find a time for you to share your experiment with the class. You may even decide to use the experiment and the results as your science fair entry this year.

Constructing Graphs

Grade Levels: 4–5

Materials Needed:

- 1 copy of Types of Graphs (p. 145)

Steps:

1. Brainstorm all of the different types of graphs you have seen. List and draw examples of each kind of graph on paper. Did you know that certain kinds of graphs are used to show certain kinds of information? Choosing the correct graph to best represent the information you have gathered is important. Considering the audience who will be studying your graph is important, too.

2. Use your favorite search engine to research "types of graphs." Locate and record information about bar graphs, line graphs, circle (pie) graphs, and pictographs.

3. Fill in the Types of Graphs chart. Be sure to list pros (good things about using the graph, such as ease of readability) and cons (things that might make the graph more difficult to use, such as it takes lots of time to create or read).

4. Brainstorm a list of fun polling questions you could ask your class. Some examples might include: favorite restaurants or foods, favorite apps, favorite electronic devices, and so on. Choose one of the polling questions and create your questionnaire. It may be easier to brainstorm choices from which students can choose rather than allowing all kinds of answers. For example, if you choose to do favorite foods, you could include five choices like pizza, hamburgers, spaghetti, shrimp and pasta, and tacos.

5. Conduct your poll and tally the results.

6. Create four different graphs to display the results of your poll.

7. Evaluate your graphs by answering the following questions:
   a. Which graph is easiest to read?
   b. Which graph was the easiest to create?
   c. Which graph does the best job showing the information you gathered?
   d. Is one graph better than the others? Explain.

8. Ask your teacher to find a time for you to share your polling results and what you learned about graphing with your class.

Types of Graphs

Directions: Research the different kinds of graphs and the information that is displayed in each. Record the information you discover in the chart below.

Types of Graphs

Type of Graph	Sketch of Graph	Pros	Cons	When Should You Use It?
Pictograph				
Bar Graph				
Circle or Pie Graph				
Line Graph				

Misleading Graphs

Grade Levels: 4–5

Materials Needed:

- 1 copy of Misleading Graphs (pp. 147–148)
- Computer with Internet access

Steps:

1. Complete the activity Constructing Graphs before beginning.
2. Use your favorite Internet search engine to research "misleading graphs." Look at some of the examples of graphs you find. Sometimes graphs are misleading because of the following problems. Try to find some of these issues in the graphs you see:
   a. no title, labels, or graph key;
   b. vertical axis doesn't start with 0;
   c. uses different sized bars or pictures; or
   d. doesn't have uniform intervals on the axes.

3. Study the graphs on the Misleading Graphs sheet and answer the questions. Keep in mind that there are ways to make all kinds of graphs misleading. Companies often use misleading graphs to make a product seem better than it is or to make sales look better (or worse) than they really are. Even politicians can use misleading graphs to their advantage. It is important to be able to spot a misleading graph so that you will not be tricked.
4. Choose one of the graphs you completed in the Constructing Graphs activity. Find ways to reconstruct the graph that make it misleading. You may use any and all of the methods you observed in your research and on the attachment.
5. Ask your teacher to find a time for you to present what you learned about misleading graphs to the class.

Misleading Graphs

Directions: Study the graph below. Circle the things that make it misleading, then answer the questions:

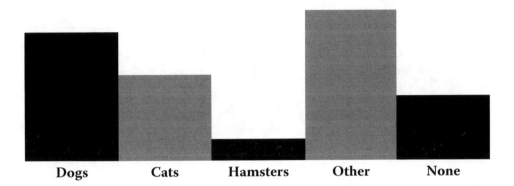

1. What do you think might be the title of this graph? Explain your answer.

    _____

    _____

    _____

2. What other titles could you have given this graph?

    _____

3. What elements of a graph are missing?

    _____

    _____

4. How could you make this graph less misleading?

    _____

    _____

    _____

Misleading Graphs, continued

Now, study the following graph and answer the questions:

Favorite Sports

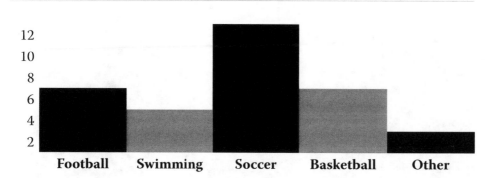

5. Is there anything misleading about this graph?

   _____

   _____

   _____

6. Redesign this graph, making it more misleading. Be sure to use the same kind of information.

Chapter 20

Cultural Borrowing Projects

Salt, Shells, and Tea Leaves

Grade Levels: 4–5

Materials Needed:

- Computer with Internet access
- Poster board
- Markers

Steps:

1. Use your favorite Internet search engine to research five ancient cultures that used objects or items instead of coins or paper money.
2. List what objects or items were used and why the items were considered valuable at that time and in that culture.
3. Imagine our country could no longer use paper and coin money and had to go back to ancient times for our monetary system. Then list what you think would be an acceptable form of currency and why.
4. Create an advertisement or display that would support your idea.
5. Ask your teacher for a time to share your ideas and research.

An Eye for an Eye

Grade Levels: 4–5

Materials Needed:

- Library access or computer with Internet access

Steps:

1. Visit the library or use your favorite Internet search engine to research Hammurabi's ancient laws.
2. Write a persuasive essay that either encourages people to return to those laws or to stay away from them.
3. Include specific examples of laws that you like or don't like.
4. Ask your teacher to find a time for you to present your essay.

The Olympic Games

Materials Needed:

- Library access
- Computer

Steps:

1. Research the ancient Greek Olympics and compare them with the modern-day Olympics. You may find books in the library about the origins of the Olympics. Create a list of sporting events from the ancient games and a short list of some of the more popular sports from today.
2. Create a Venn diagram to compare the modern and ancient Olympics.
3. Identify the cultural aspects from Ancient Greece that remain in our modern-day Olympics.
4. Describe how countries that host the Olympics get to showcase their culture.
5. Make a PowerPoint presentation that shows the following information:
   a. the history of the Olympic games,
   b. how the modern Olympics are similar to and different from the ancient Olympics, and
   c. how host countries share their culture with the world.

6. Ask your teacher to find a time for you to share your PowerPoint presentation with the class.

Spreading the Culture

Grade Levels: 4–5

Materials Needed:

- Library access or computer with Internet access

Steps:

1. Use your favorite Internet search engine or visit the library to research the Silk Road or Silk Route.
2. Create a map showing the 4,000-mile land and sea routes.
3. Identify at least 10 goods and technologies that were traded on these routes.
4. Identify at least two religions or philosophies that were passed along on this route.
5. Write an essay explaining how the Silk Road was significant in the development of great civilizations like China, India, Ancient Egypt, Persia, Arabia, and Ancient Rome and what finally stopped the Silk Road in the 1400s.
6. Ask your teacher to find a time for you to present your essay to the class.

Chapter 21

Advertisements and Labels Projects

Are All Breads Created Equal?

Grade Levels: 4–5

Materials Needed:

- Packaging from two different kinds of breads that are advertised for being healthy choices
- Computer with Internet access

Steps:

1. Examine the nutrition facts labels and packaging claims on two brands of bread. Create a chart comparing the following information:
   a. calories per serving (be sure to check whether the serving is one or two slices),
   b. fat grams per serving,
   c. percent of daily value of iron,
   d. milligrams of sodium,
   e. total grams of carbohydrates,
   f. grams of dietary fiber,
   g. grams of sugar,
   h. grams of protein, and
   i. the first ingredient on the ingredients list.

2. What claims, if any, does the company make on the packaging? How does the company let you know it believes its bread is a healthy choice? Write a paragraph about each kind of bread, describing what each company does to entice health-conscious people to purchase its product.

3. Use your favorite Internet search engine to research the following question: "How do I choose a healthy bread?" Click on several articles and take notes about what you find. You should discover that breads with 100% wheat, with whole-wheat flour, and with low amounts of sodium are the healthiest to eat.

4. Using what you have learned from your research and comparing the nutrition facts labels, decide which bread is the healthiest. Write a paragraph explaining why one bread is healthier than the other.

5. Ask your teacher to find a time for you to share your nutrition information with the class.

Being a Good Consumer

|||||||||||||||||||||||||||||||||||||||||||||||||||||||||||||||||||||||||||||||||||||||||||||||||||||||||||||||||||||||||||||||||||||||||||||||||||||||||||||||||||||

Grade Levels: 4–5

Materials Needed:

- Computer with Internet access
- 1 poster board or piece of chart paper

Steps:

1. Use an online dictionary to help you define "consumer" as it relates to business.
2. Brainstorm a list of your favorite toy commercials. What products are being sold? How much do the products cost? Is it possible for people to get hurt if they use them?
3. Think about how you know something is a good deal. What do you think the phrase "good deal" means? Brainstorm a list of conditions a product should meet to make it a good deal. This could include properties such as sturdy, convenient size, not too expensive, and so on. Remember, buying something because it is the least expensive is often not the best choice. A good consumer always has to consider the quality of the product.
4. Think of one toy you have owned for several years that you think was a good deal. Draw a picture of this product and create a list of all of its redeeming qualities. Was this toy ever advertised? What about the advertisement caused you to want to buy this toy? Write a paragraph that explains how this toy was a good deal.
5. Think of another toy that you owned that was not a good deal. What happened to make you think this toy did not turn out to be what was promised? Was this toy ever advertised? What about the advertisement caused you to want to buy this toy? Are there other similar toys that might have been better than this one? Write a paragraph that explains the reasons why this toy was a bad deal.
6. Watch television on a children's station several times over 3 days. Take notes on every toy commercial you see.
7. Choose three toys to research. Use the commercial and the Internet to get information about each product.
8. Create a poster that has a picture of each product, tells about each product, and includes the price of each product.
9. Create a presentation using your poster as a visual. As a part of your presentation, be sure to explain why you would or would not buy each product.
10. Ask your teacher to find a time for you to present your work to the class.

Advertising Techniques

Materials Needed:

- Several magazines
- 1 copy of Advertising Techniques (pp. 157–158)
- Computer with Internet access

Steps:

1. Brainstorm a list of your favorite advertisements (from TV, the Internet, or print). List the characteristics of each advertisement that appeal to you the most. For example, is the ad accompanied by a catchy jingle? Does the ad make you want to go and purchase the product?

2. Marketing specialists use many advertising techniques to get consumers in their stores or to visit their websites. The techniques they employ depend on the audience to which they are marketing. It is our job, as consumers, to be informed and to realize these techniques are being used to change our thinking about a product or service.

3. Use your favorite Internet search engine and a copy of the Advertising Techniques sheet to research some of the more common advertising techniques marketing specialists use to convince consumers to use their product or service.

4. Choose your favorite ad from the brainstormed list. If it is a TV ad, write the script for the ad and make a list of all of the images the ad uses. You can use the Internet to find a sample commercial or to check whether a specific commercial can be viewed online. You may also choose to peruse a magazine to find an ad to use.

5. Identify as many of the advertising techniques as you can in the ad you chose. Answer the following questions after you have examined the ad:
   a. What audience was the ad trying to appeal to? Children? Teenagers? The elderly? Parents of young children?
   b. Did the ad use each advertising technique effectively?
   c. Was there another technique you thought might have worked better for the targeted audience and why?

6. Choose a unique way to present the information you have uncovered about advertising. You may choose to find examples of every advertising technique you researched and demonstrate them in a presentation style of your choice. Be sure to explain the different kinds of techniques and tell about how they are employed in your favorite ad.

7. Ask your teacher to find a time for you to present your advertising knowledge to the class.

Advertising Techniques

Directions: Research the several kinds of advertising techniques below, then record your findings on this chart.

Name of Technique	Definition of Technique	Audience This Technique Might Appeal to	Example of Technique in Use
Bribery	The use of this technique gives the consumer something extra, in addition to the product or service.	Everyone. Who doesn't like something for free?	But wait, if you buy now, we'll double your order and send two packages of _____ for one low price!
Snob Appeal			
Plain Folks			
Testimonial			

Advertising Techniques, continued

Name of Technique	Definition of Technique	Audience This Technique Might Appeal to	Example of Technique in Use
Card Stacking			
Celebrity Endorsement			
Bandwagon			
Emotional Appeal			

Sell! Sell! Sell!

Materials Needed:

- You will need to complete the Advertising Techniques activity before you can complete this activity.

Steps:

1. Brainstorm a list of products in which you think your friends might be interested. Choose one product and write a description of it. Be sure to list important characteristics that might appeal to a student like you. For example, "My product is a new kind of candy bar. It has a center of marshmallows surrounded by crunchy peanuts, dipped in caramel, and covered in chocolate, then coated in a candy shell."
2. Create a catchy name for your product.
3. Think about how you will advertise your product. Who will be the audience of your advertisement? What advertising techniques will you use to sell your product? Use the Advertising Techniques chart from the last activity to help you create your commercial, magazine ad, or online pop-up ad for your product.
4. Design the packaging for your new product. Try to incorporate at least one advertising technique into the packaging.
5. Write a paragraph telling about your product and the advertising techniques you used in your marketing.
6. Ask your teacher to find a time for you to present your new product, the ad, the packaging, and the paragraph about advertising techniques you employed with the class.

Chapter 22

Geography Utopia Projects

Utopia

||||||||||||||||||||||||||||||||||||||||||||||||||||||||||||||||||||||||||||||||||||||||||||||||||

Grade Levels: 4–5

Materials Needed:

- Poster board
- Markers

Steps:

1. Imagine a perfect place on Earth where everyone lives in harmony with one another and with nature. Some people refer to this type of place as a utopia.
2. Create the geography of your perfect country—what would you imagine? List the geographic features you would include in your utopia such as lakes, rivers, mountains, deserts, deltas, and so on.
3. Draw the shape of your country on your poster board. It could be a circle, square, or anything you think would make for a perfect country.
4. Become a cartographer and create a physical map showing the identifiable geographic features you listed. Water is usually shown in blue. Colors are used to show relief—differences in land elevations. Green is typically used at lower elevations, and orange or brown indicate higher elevations. Visit the library and examine some of the globes there. Some of them will have raised areas that indicate mountainous regions of Earth.
5. Ask your teacher to give you an appropriate place to display your map.

Climate and Weather in Utopia

Materials Needed:

- None

Steps:

1. Imagine a perfect place on Earth. What type of climate will your utopia have? Will it be the same all over the country, or have different climate regions?
2. Decide what your average precipitation and temperature will be per month in the different regions.
3. Examine a social studies textbook and look for charts that show the average precipitation and temperatures for a region. Create similar charts for your utopia that show the average precipitation and temperature you will have each month in each region.
4. List the crops each region will be able to produce according to climate and precipitation.
5. Ask your teacher to give you an appropriate place to display your climate and precipitation charts.

Natural Resources

Grade Levels: 4–5

Materials Needed:

- Poster board
- Markers

Steps:

1. Decide what types of natural resources you will have in your utopia and which ones you will or will not use. For example, if you use oil, natural gas deposits, or coal, will you choose to ignore them for the sake of the environment or will you use them in ways that will make your country environmentally friendly yet productive?
2. Create a natural resources map of your utopia and identify where the natural resources are located.
3. Draw symbols to label each kind of resource.
4. Create a map key to show how each resource is represented. For example, if you identified oil as a resource, you might draw an oil derrick to represent each oil deposit.
5. Ask your teacher to give you an appropriate place to display your map.

The One and Only

Materials Needed:

- Poster board or large index card
- Markers

Steps:

1. Imagine a new land or water form. It is only found in your new country. For example, this new landform could be called the natural slide and be located on the side of a mountain and people could slide down it to quickly move from the top to the bottom of the mountain area.
2. Describe the new land or water form.
3. Draw an illustration of what it would look like so visitors to your country can identify it.
4. Identify, then list, the pros and cons of this new land or water form.
5. Ask your teacher to give you an appropriate time to explain your new land or water form.

Chapter 23

Alternate Energy Forms Projects

Wondering About Wind Power

Materials Needed:

- Library access or computer with Internet access

Steps:

1. Visit the library or use your favorite Internet search engine to research how electricity is made using wind power. Try to answer the following questions as you research:
   a. Is this form of energy renewable or nonrenewable?
   b. How do we use this energy source to make electricity?
   c. Does making electricity using this source cause pollution?
   d. Is this energy source always available someplace on Earth?
   e. What areas on Earth are the best for using this energy source to produce electricity?
   f. What are the pros of using this energy source to produce electricity?
   g. What are the cons of using this energy source to produce electricity?
   h. How is this energy source being used today to generate electricity?
   i. How do you think this energy source will be used in 50 years to generate electricity?

2. Create an informative PowerPoint presentation about wind power as an alternate energy source. You may want to complete research on the remainder of the Alternate Energy Forms Projects in this chapter and include a slide at the end of the presentation comparing the other energy sources to wind power.

3. Ask your teacher to find a time for you to show your PowerPoint presentation to the class.

Have You Heard About Hydroelectric?

Grade Levels: 4–5

Materials Needed:

- Library access or computer with Internet access

Steps:

1. Visit the library or use your favorite Internet search engine to research how electricity is made using hydroelectric power. Try to answer the following questions as you research:
   a. Is this form of energy renewable or nonrenewable?
   b. How do we use this energy source to make electricity?
   c. Does making electricity using this source cause pollution?
   d. Is this energy source always available someplace on Earth?
   e. What areas on Earth are the best for using this energy source to produce electricity?
   f. What are the pros of using this energy source to produce electricity?
   g. What are the cons of using this energy source to produce electricity?
   h. How is this energy source being used today to generate electricity?
   i. How do you think this energy source will be used in 50 years to generate electricity?

2. Create an informative Glogster poster about hydroelectric power as an alternate energy source. You may want to complete research on the remainder of the Alternate Energy Forms Projects in the rest of this chapter and include information comparing the other energy sources to hydroelectric power.
3. Ask your teacher to find a time for you to show your poster to the class.

Solar Power

Grade Levels: 4–5

Materials Needed:

- Library access or computer with Internet access

Steps:

1. Visit the library or use your favorite Internet search engine to research how electricity is made using solar power. Try to answer the following questions as you research:
   a. Is this form of energy renewable or nonrenewable?
   b. How do we use this energy source to make electricity?
   c. Does making electricity using this source cause pollution?
   d. Is this energy source always available someplace on Earth?
   e. What areas on Earth are the best for using this energy source to produce electricity?
   f. What are the pros of using this energy source to produce electricity?
   g. What are the cons of using this energy source to produce electricity?
   h. How is this energy source being used today to generate electricity?
   i. How do you think this energy source will be used in 50 years to generate electricity?

2. Create an informative Prezi presentation about solar power as an alternate energy source. You may want to complete research on the remainder of the Alternate Energy Forms Projects found in the rest of this chapter and include information comparing the other energy sources to solar power.
3. Ask your teacher to find a time for you to show your Prezi presentation to the class.

Geothermal Power

Materials Needed:

- Library access or computer with Internet access

Steps:

1. Visit the library or use your favorite Internet search engine to research how electricity is made using geothermal power. Try to answer the following questions as you research:
    a. Is this form of energy renewable or nonrenewable?
    b. How do we use this energy source to make electricity?
    c. Does making electricity using this source cause pollution?
    d. Is this energy source always available someplace on Earth?
    e. What areas on Earth are the best for using this energy source to produce electricity?
    f. What are the pros of using this energy source to produce electricity?
    g. What are the cons of using this energy source to produce electricity?
    h. How is this energy source being used today to generate electricity?
    i. How do you think this energy source will be used in 50 years to generate electricity?

2. Create an informative presentation in a style of your choosing about geothermal power as an alternate energy source. You may want to complete research on the remainder of the Alternate Energy Forms Projects found in the rest of this chapter and include information in your project comparing the other energy sources to geothermal power.

3. Ask your teacher to find a time for you to present your project to the class.

Chapter 24
Immigration Projects

Immigration Policies

Materials Needed:

- Computer with Internet access

Steps:

1. Understand that most countries have a policy that helps control the number of people immigrating, or moving, to their country each year. Use your favorite Internet search engine to help you discover the immigration policies in at least three countries such as Ireland, Canada, Israel, China, Japan, Switzerland, and so on. Record your research on notebook paper.

2. Create an immigration policy you would like to see in a new country that you establish. Use some of the information you gathered about the three countries you researched to help you make decisions about your policies.

3. Explain your policy and the reasons you made it by writing a three-paragraph essay. Be sure to reference the countries you researched as the inspiration for your immigration policies.

4. Ask your teacher to help you find an appropriate time to present your finished product.

Angel Island vs. Ellis Island

Grade Levels: 4–5

Materials Needed:

- Computer with Internet access
- Notebook paper

Steps:

1. Recognize that not every immigrant came to America by way of the East Coast. From 1910 to 1940, Angel Island in San Francisco processed hundreds of thousands of immigrants, the majority of whom came from China.

2. Use your favorite Internet search engine to research the history of Angel Island from 1910 to 1940. Take notes on the way immigrants were processed at that entry point.

3. Research Ellis Island during that same time period.

4. Fold a piece of notebook paper in half. Open it up and label one side "Immigrants at Angel Island" and the other side "Immigrants at Ellis Island."

5. Take notes to compare and contrast the treatment and processing of the immigrants at Ellis Island and the immigrants at Angel Island.

6. Write a four-paragraph essay explaining what you learned about the similarities and differences between the treatment of immigrants at Ellis Island and those who arrived at Angel Island. Your first paragraph should introduce your subject. The second paragraph should tell how the experiences of the immigrants were similar. The third paragraph should explain how the experiences of the immigrants were different. The fourth paragraph should restate your main points and bring your writing to a close.

7. Share your essay with one or two classmates and make revisions according to their constructive feedback.

8. Create a final copy of your essay.

9. Ask your teacher to help you find an appropriate time to present your finished product.

Entrance Denied

Materials Needed:

- Computer with Internet access
- Notebook paper

Steps:

1. Understand that not all countries take in refugees or accept immigrants, even in emergency or temporary situations. On notebook paper, brainstorm and list reasons you think some countries refuse to take in immigrants.
2. Select three countries (one country in Asia, one country in Europe, and one country in Africa), plus Canada and Australia, and research whether or not they accept immigrants and, if so, under what circumstances. Take notes on all five countries and include any statistical data you find. You will need to use your favorite Internet search engine to explore these questions and details.
3. Select one of these five countries and write a procedural text that explains what steps you would have to take in order to gain citizenship.
4. Share your writing with one or two classmates and make revisions according to their constructive feedback.
5. Create a final copy of your writing.
6. Ask your teacher to help you find an appropriate time to present or display your finished product.

What Do You Know?

Materials Needed:

- Computer with Internet access

Steps:

1. Test yourself by writing down what you think the steps are in order to apply for American citizenship.
2. Use your favorite Internet search engine to research the documentation, money, and time necessary to apply for citizenship.
3. Research what steps are required to go through the citizenship process.
4. Compare and contrast what you thought to what you found.
5. In order to become a United States citizen, applicants must pass a test. Use your favorite Internet search engine to search "citizenship quiz." Click on one of the links and take a sample quiz. Do you know the answers to all of the questions? How difficult was the quiz for you? How difficult do you think the test is for someone moving here from a foreign country?
6. Make a presentation that will be informative and entertaining for the class. You might include some of the more interesting or challenging questions from the citizenship quiz as part of your presentation.

Chapter 25

Westward Expansion Projects

Don't Leave Home Without It!

Grade Levels: 4–5

Materials Needed:

- Art paper
- Markers or paint
- Computer with Internet access

Steps:

1. In 1859, a book was published entitled *The Prairie Traveler: A Handbook for Overland Expeditions* written by Randolph B. Marcy. It was used by those daring settlers and adventurers who decided to join the Western expansion of America. This book is considered a primary source, and historians have used it to uncover some of the questions arising from how travelers made this trek successfully.
2. Go to your favorite Internet search engine and find a copy of *The Prairie Traveler: A Handbook for Overland Expeditions*, or go to a website like http://www.kancoll.org/books/marcy.
3. Select a chapter in the book to read in depth.

4. Make a list of at least 10 words that were used in the book that are rarely used or not generally understood by Americans today such as desiccated, egress, ingress, tentfly, terminus, ply, and so on.

5. Copy the sentence in which each word is used. For example, desiccated means dehydrated; it comes from the following sentence in Chapter 1, "Desiccated or dried vegetables are almost equal to the fresh . . . " The context clues in this example make the meaning of the word clear. If context clues do not help the reader understand the meaning of the word, then create and write a sentence that would make the word clear.

6. Define the words that you think would be helpful for somebody reading and using that chapter today in order to duplicate what settlers had to do in order to move westward.

Which Way?

Grade Levels: 4–5

Materials Needed:

- 1 copy of Pros and Cons (p. 178)
- Computer with Internet access

Steps:

- Go to your favorite Internet search engine and find a copy of *The Prairie Traveler: A Handbook for Overland Expeditions*, or go to a website like http://www.kancoll.org/books/marcy.
- Read Chapter 1 of *The Prairie Traveler: A Handbook for Overland Expeditions*.
- Use the Pros and Cons sheet to name each route west with a name that makes sense to you. Take notes listing the pros and cons of each of the routes described in this chapter.
- Analyze the information you recorded, then identify which route you would take.
- Create a written report that identifies the route you selected and your reasons for making that selection. Be sure to include the time of year you would begin your expedition.
- Draw a map of the route you would follow using the landmarks of 1859.
- Ask your teacher to find a time for you to present your map and report to the class.

Pros and Cons

Directions: Read the first chapter of *The Prairie Traveler: A Handbook for Overland Expeditions* and give each Western route a name that makes sense. List the name of each route in the chart below. Then list the pros and cons of each route you found.

Route Name	Pros	Cons

Interesting Facts

Grade Levels: 4–5

Materials Needed:

- Computer with Internet access

Steps:

1. Go to your favorite Internet search engine and find a copy of *A Handbook for Overland Expeditions* written by Randolph B. Marcy, first published in 1859, or go to a website like http://www.kancoll.org/books/marcy.
2. Skim and scan *A Handbook for Overland Expeditions*.
3. Record at least 10 interesting facts you discover. For example, wagon wheels would be taken off and soaked in a river or pond overnight. That would swell the wood temporarily and make the wheels stronger.
4. Display the facts in an interesting way. One interesting way you could show the information would be to create a "Did You Know?" poster with illustrations.
5. Ask your teacher to find a time for you to share the facts you found with the class.

Chapter 26

Rocks and Earth Projects

Classifying Rocks

Grade Levels: 4–5

Materials Needed:

- A collection of rocks
- 1 copy of Classifying Rocks (p. 183)

Steps:

1. Choose seven different rocks from the collection. Examine the rocks and note each rock's unique characteristics. Write a description of each rock on a sheet of paper.
2. Choose three more rocks and add them to the seven you described. Give your rock descriptions to a friend and see whether he or she can match the rocks you used with the descriptions you wrote. Do not share which rocks you actually described. Be sure to explain that there are three extra rocks in the group as distractors. Was your friend able to identify each of the rocks by the descriptions you wrote?
3. When scientists classify items, they use very specific vocabulary and consider all physical characteristics. This is necessary so that when a scientist thinks he or she has discovered a new rock, animal, or mineral, research can be done to see whether the new thing has ever been described and named before.
4. Scientists have all kinds of ways to classify rocks and minerals. Use the Classifying Rocks sheet to help you get an idea of the characteristics

scientists consider as they study, describe, and classify rocks. Classify the same rocks you described earlier.

5. Now that you have classified the rocks using the descriptions on the Classifying Rocks sheet, rewrite the description of each rock using some of the scientific descriptions on the sheet. Add several more rocks to the seven you described. Give your new descriptions to your friend and see whether she can match the new descriptions to your original rocks. Your friend likely did better the second time because your descriptions were written more scientifically.

6. Ask your teacher to find a time for you to present your descriptions and classification materials to the class.

Classifying Rocks

Directions: Classify each rock you found using the scientific observations below. Then rewrite your original descriptions of each rock below, using more scientific vocabulary in your descriptions.

Rock Found	Rough or Smooth?	Heavy or Light?	What Color Is It?	Does It Have Spots? Stripes?	Shiny or Dull?	Magnetic or Nonmagnetic?	Conductor or Insulator?

Igneous, Metamorphic, and Sedimentary Rocks

Grade Levels: 4–5

Materials Needed:

- Library access or computer with Internet access

Steps:

1. Visit the library or use your favorite Internet search engine to discover three different classifications of rocks: igneous, metamorphic, and sedimentary. Try to answer the following questions:
   a. How is this kind of rock formed?
   b. Where is this rock formed?
   c. Where can you find this rock on Earth?
   d. What are some examples of this kind of rock? (Save pictures of the rocks if you find them.)

2. Create a PowerPoint presentation that shows how and where each kind of rock is formed, where you can find the rocks on Earth, and examples of some of the rocks.

3. Try to find some of the rocks you listed in your PowerPoint. For instance, you may be able to find a piece of lava rock (an igneous rock) in a barbecue grill because it can help even the heat distribution inside the grill. You may be able to find a piece of granite (a metamorphic rock) at a countertop store because many people have countertops made from granite. You can also ask your teacher or friends for help locating rock samples.

4. Write a song to teach the difference between igneous, metamorphic, and sedimentary rocks. You may choose to complete the sample song below, writing two more stanzas for igneous and metamorphic rocks, or write a new song of your own.

   My Rock Song
   (to the tune of "Amazing Grace")
   Amazing rock, you sit right there.
   You formed for cen-tur-ies.
   While sand and dirt pressed down on you,
   I call you sedi-men-tary.

5. Ask your teacher to find a time for you to present your PowerPoint presentation and song to the class.

Wind, Water, and Ice

Grade Levels: 4–5

Materials Needed:

- Computer with Internet access
- Paper
- Markers
- Computer printer

Steps:

1. Explore the following websites of four national parks to learn about some of the most unique landforms in the world:
   a. Arches National Park in Utah: http://www.nps.gov/arch/index.htm
   b. Bryce Canyon National Park in Utah: http://www.nps.gov/brca/index.htm
   c. Grand Canyon National Park in Arizona: http://www.nps.gov/grca/index.htm
   d. White Sands National Monument in New Mexico: http://www.nps.gov/whsa/index.htm

2. Try to answer the following questions as you research the parks:
   a. How were the unique features in each park formed (by wind, water, ice, or combination of the three)?
   b. What kinds of rocks are the unique features made from (sedimentary, igneous, metamorphic)?
   c. What are some unique features inside the park? (Save some pictures for later.)
   d. How is the park being protected?
   e. What are some interesting things tourists can do at the park?
   f. When can tourists visit the park?

3. Use the information you gathered to create a trifold travel brochure about one of the parks. You can use a publishing program to create your brochure online, or use paper and markers to create a handmade brochure. Print pictures from the websites to include in your handmade brochure.
4. Be sure to include information in your brochure about how the park was formed and what geologic processes are at work.
5. Ask your teacher to set a time for you to present your brochure to the class.

Fossil Fuels

Grade Levels: 4–5

Materials Needed:

- 1 long sheet of chart paper
- Computer with Internet access

Steps:

1. Use your favorite Internet search engine to research fossil fuels. Try to answer the following questions as you read:
   a. What are the three main forms of fossil fuels?
   b. When were they formed?
   c. Are fossil fuels a renewable source of energy? Why or why not?
   d. Where are the deposits of each fossil fuel found in the United States?
   e. How is the fossil fuel mined?
   f. How is the fossil fuel refined and transported?
   g. Why is the world so dependent on fossil fuels?
   h. Why is it so important to conserve fossil fuels?

2. Choose one fossil fuel that interests you. Draw and label a long flow chart that shows the process of how the fossil fuel formed and the steps we take to mine and refine it into a usable energy source.
3. Ask your teacher to find a time for you to present your flow chart to the class.

Chapter 27

Forms of Government Projects

My Perfect Form of Government

Grade Levels: 4–5

Materials Needed:

- Computer with Internet access

Steps:

1. Imagine you had the power to start a new country in the world and could decide the form of government you would have.
2. Use your favorite Internet search engine to help you define the following forms of government: dictatorship, totalitarian, theocracy, monarchy, parliamentary, and democracy.
3. Write a brief description of each and the name of a country that is run this way today.
4. Decide on the type of government system you think will work best in your new country. You can use one of those defined, a combination of two or more, or create your own form of government and give it a name.
5. Create a graphic organizer that shows how your form of government will work. For example, the United States uses a system of checks and balances in our democratic government, with three branches of government so no one part can be more powerful than the other two. The

graphic organizer can be shown as an equilateral triangle, with each side being exactly the same, showing that the power of each part of the government is the same.

6. Write a persuasive speech explaining why this is the perfect system of government for your new country.

7. Ask your teacher to help you find an appropriate time to present your speech to the class.

Despots

Materials Needed:

- Computer with Internet access

Steps:

1. Use an online dictionary to help you define despot with regard to government leadership.
2. List synonyms and antonyms of despot.
3. Research and identify at least five despots.
4. Describe how they ruled and what became of them.
5. Make a PowerPoint or any other presentation of your choosing to convey the information you found.
6. Ask your teacher to find a time for you to present your information to the class.

Why "The Great"?

Grade Levels: 4–5

Materials Needed:

- Computer with Internet access

Steps:

1. Use your favorite Internet search engine to research a list of rulers who had "the Great" added to their names such as Alexander the Great, Catherine the Great, and Frederick the Great.
2. Narrow your list to five by classifying them as the most beloved, most ruthless, or other word that describes their character.
3. Write a reader's theater, skit, or mock interview that introduces your characters and explains how or why he or she received that title.
4. Ask some friends to help you practice the script you created and have your teacher find a time you can present your play to the class.

The French Revolution

Materials Needed:

- Computer with Internet access

Steps:

1. Use your favorite Internet search engine to research how the French Revolution (1789–1799) violently transformed France.
2. Create a graphic organizer, such as a T-chart, that lists what France was like before, then after, the Revolution.
3. Find several well-known paintings by French artists created during the French Revolution that illustrate your research.
4. Use the art in a presentation style of your choosing to tell the story of before, during, and after the revolution. Use background music to set the mood and better convey the story. (The French national anthem, *La Marseillaise*, was composed during this time period and would be a great audio addition to the presentation.)
5. Ask your teacher to find a time for you to present your presentation to the class.

Chapter 28
Earth and Space Projects

Weather vs. Climate

Materials Needed:

- Library access

Steps:

1. Visit the library and check out books about weather and climate. Read the books to help you differentiate between weather and climate.
2. Create a T-chart. On one side of the T-chart, write "Weather." Write "Climate" on the other side of the chart. Sort the following observations into the "weather" or "climate" columns on your T-chart:
   a. The average annual temperature in Texas has risen 2 degrees over the last 30 years.
   b. Two inches of rain have been reported in the past week.
   c. The wind is currently blowing from the northwest at 5 miles per hour.
   d. Rainfall patterns have steadily decreased over the Southwestern United States since the 1970s.
   e. Areas in the Northeastern United States receive more snow, on average, than people in the Southwest.
   f. Tornado watches and warnings are common in April and May in Texas and Oklahoma.
   g. Dallas, TX, received more than 5 inches of rain in January.

3. Write and illustrate a short children's book that explains the difference between weather and climate. You may even want to create a quiz similar to the one above to be sure students understand the difference.

4. Ask your teacher to find a time for you to present your book to the class. You may wish to ask permission to read your book to a younger class or display your book in the library.

Layers of the Earth and Atmosphere

Grade Levels: 4–5

Materials Needed:

- Six different colors of clay
- 1 large piece of chart paper
- Colored pencils or markers
- Computer with Internet access

Steps:

1. Use your favorite Internet search engine to research the layers of the Earth. Draw and label a picture of the inside of the Earth, noting the relative thickness of each layer to the others.
2. After the lithosphere layer, comes the atmosphere where we live and breathe. There are five layers to Earth's atmosphere before it touches space. Research and draw a picture of the layers of Earth's atmosphere, noting the relative thickness of each layer to the others.
3. Use modeling clay to build a model of the layers of the Earth.
4. Attach your model Earth to the center of the piece of chart paper. Draw, label, and color in the layers of the atmosphere around the model Earth using large circles. Label the layers of the Earth using small pieces of paper.
5. Research the meanings of the following prefixes to help you remember the different layers of the atmosphere and topmost layers of the Earth: astheno-, litho-, tropo-, strato-, meso-, thermo-, and exo-. Record this information on your chart paper.
6. Ask your teacher to help you find a time to present your project to the class.

Plate Tectonics

||||||||||||||||||||||||||||||||||||||||||||||||||||||||||||||||||||||||||||||||||||||||||||||||||||||||||||||||||||||||||||||||||||||

Materials Needed:

- Computer with Internet access
- World map
- Colored pencils

Steps:

1. Use your favorite Internet search engine to research plate tectonics. Try to answer the following questions as you read:
   a. Who first developed the theory of continental drift?
   b. What was Pangaea?
   c. How are the continents of Earth like a puzzle?
   d. Why are Earth's continents in motion? What forces under the lithosphere are at work?
   e. How is new crust formed on Earth? What happens to old crust in the depths of the oceans?
   f. What happens when the plates collide or separate?

2. Scientists have studied the surface of the Earth, including the ocean floor. They have discovered that the surface of the Earth is broken into several large plates and many smaller plates that move together. Get a copy of a world map from your teacher. Use your favorite Internet search engine to research the locations of the following tectonic plates: Eurasian, African, Indo-Australian, Pacific, North American, and South American. Draw, color, and label these plates on your map.

3. Study the map you created and predict where you think earthquakes and volcanoes might be present based on the locations of the tectonic plates.

4. Ask your teacher to find a time for you to present your map to the class.

Plate Tectonics and Geological Events

Grade Levels: 4–5

Materials Needed:

- Library access
- Computer with Internet access

Steps:

1. Visit the library and find books about one of the following topics: earthquakes, volcanoes, or mountains.
2. Read to understand the geological processes that were involved in causing these geological events. Try to answer the following questions as you read:
   a. How does plate tectonics help cause this geological event?
   b. What things must happen in the Earth for this event to occur?
   c. Is this geological event related to other geological events (for example, volcanic eruptions are often preceded and followed by earthquakes)?

3. Research some noteworthy geological events related to your topic. For instance, what are some of the most active volcanoes in the world? What were the five most destructive earthquakes on record? Which mountain is the tallest in the world, and how was it formed?
4. Try to locate pictures of the noteworthy geological events in the step above. Create a Glogster mash-up of photographs that help explain the geological processes that cause the topic you chose. Include the pictures you found of the noteworthy events.
5. Ask your teacher to find a time for you to present your Glogster mash-up.

Chapter 29

Five Themes of Geography Projects

Country Report

Grade Levels: 4–5

Materials Needed:

- 1 copy of The Five Themes of Geography Country Report (p. 201)
- Colored pencils
- Computer with Internet access

Steps:

1. Use your favorite Internet search engine to locate a video or PowerPoint presentation that clearly explains the five themes of geography. This website should be approved by your teacher. Two suggestions are provided:
   a. http://video.about.com/geography/Five-Themes-of-Geography.htm
   b. http://geography.mrdonn.org/powerpoints/5themes.html

2. Select a country or region to research that you know little about such as Zambia, Wales, Turkey, Falkland Islands, Lithuania, and so on.

3. Take notes on The Five Themes of Geography Country Report to collect information about the country.

---

4. Compile your notes into a written report that tells about the country through the five themes of geography.

5. Locate and print or sketch a map of the country, identifying the capital, the major mountain ranges and rivers, and any large bodies of water nearby. Color your map. Be sure to add a map key, compass rose, and title for your map.

6. Ask your teacher to find a time for you to present your report and map to the class.

The Five Themes of Geography Country Report

Name of Country:_____

1. **Location:** Where is it on Earth?

   _____

2. **Place:** What does it look like? What makes it different and interesting?

   _____

3. **Human and Environmental Relationships:** Why did people settle here? Pollution? Population growth?

   _____

   _____

   _____

4. **Movement, Human Interactions:** How do people get around? History? Imports & Exports?

   _____

   _____

   _____

5. **Region:** Do some areas naturally go together? (Remember, there can be more than one way to define regions.)

   _____

   _____

   _____

Location, Location, Location

Grade Levels: 4–5

Materials Needed:

- World map or globe
- Computer with Internet access

Steps:

1. Use a world map to locate a country that you have no prior knowledge about.

2. Make a written prediction about how the people living in this location adapted to the physical environment using only physical and political maps. For example, you might choose a country that is located closer to the North Pole than the equator such as Norway. How do you think the people have adapted to live in such a cold climate? Do they grow food or import it? What do you think this country exports to help it grow economically?

3. Research the country and see how accurate your prediction was.

4. Write a report comparing and contrasting your prediction with actual facts.

5. Ask your teacher to find a time for you to present your report to the class.

Cause and Effect

||||||||||||||||||||||||||||||||||||||||||||||||||||||||||||||||||||||||||||||||||||||||||||||||||||||||||||||||||||||||||||||||||||||||||||||||||||||||||||||||

Grade Levels: 4–5

Materials Needed:

- World map
- Poster board
- Colored pencils

Steps:

1. Use a world map in your social studies book to locate a country that has an abundance of natural resources.
2. Research how the natural resources have affected the country's growth with regard to population, pollution, education, and economics and stability of the country. For example, are the largest cities located near the most lucrative natural resources? A country that identifies coastal fishing as one of its major natural resources may have major cities located at strategic areas on its coastline.
3. Write a short report that explains the settlement patterns of people in the country based on its natural resources.
4. Create a large map of the country you chose, identifying all of the natural resources you researched. Be sure to title the map, label the major cities and the capitol, and identify any major rivers, mountain ranges, and large bodies of water. Color your map and include a compass rose and map key.
5. Ask your teacher for a time when you can share your report and map with the class.

Can You Sing It?

Grade Levels: 4–5

Materials Needed:

- Video camera
- Computer with Internet access

Steps:

1. Use your favorite Internet search engine to locate a video or PowerPoint presentation that clearly explains the five themes of geography. This website should be approved by your teacher. Two suggestions are provided:
   a. http://video.about.com/geography/Five-Themes-of-Geography.htm
   b. http://geography.mrdonn.org/powerpoints/5themes.html

2. Write a rap or catchy tune that will help students to learn the five themes of geography.
3. Create a set of helpful visuals to go with your song.
4. Record your song using a video camera and the visuals you created.
5. Ask your teacher to find a time for you to share your video with the class.

Chapter 30

Economic Systems Projects

Economic Systems Debate

||||||||||||||||||||||||||||||||||||||||||||||||||||||||||||||||||||||||||||||||||||||||||||||||||||||||||||||||||||||||||||

Grade Levels: 4–5

Materials Needed:

- Computer with Internet access

Steps:

1. Use your favorite Internet search engine to help you research the parts of a debate. Be sure to define the following parts: the affirmative side, negative side, moderator, opening, first rebuttal, second rebuttal, and closing.
2. Use your favorite Internet search engine to research three of the most well-known economic systems: capitalism, communism, and socialism.
3. Take notes comparing and contrasting these three economic systems.
4. Prepare a scripted debate that argues for using each economic system. You can use a search engine to look for sample debate scripts to help you get started. In this type of debate, the moderator poses questions for each speaker to answer such as:

   Moderator: Could each of the speakers, #1, #2, and #3, give a brief definition of your economic system?

Differentiated Projects for Gifted Students © Prufrock Press Inc.

Permission is granted to photocopy or reproduce this page for single classroom use only.

205

5. Ask three classmates to rehearse the scripted debate you wrote.

6. Ask your teacher when you and your classmates can present the debate to the class.

7. Note: It is important that the speakers and moderator remain objective and give facts without interjecting persuasive techniques or actually using the name of the economic system they represent.

8. Ask the audience to identify which economic system they liked best, #1, #2, or #3, and why.

9. Give students an opportunity to write their answers. Introduce the speakers as either representing the capitalism, communism, or socialism. If necessary, point out that the United States has a capitalist economic system.

10. Invite students to share their writing and thoughts.

Bartering

Materials Needed:

- None

Steps:

1. Understand that barter or bartering is a method of exchange by which no money is used. Goods or services are exchanged for other goods or services. That is a simple process if the two parties feel that the exchange is fair. For example, Person #1 has two footballs and no baseballs. Person #2 has two baseballs but no footballs. They each have a desire to own one of each. That would be a fair trade.

2. Imagine a scenario where Person #1 has 2 footballs and 2 baseballs but wants a baseball bat. Person #1 can find plenty of people who have baseball bats but nobody wants what he has to trade (1 football and 1 baseball).

3. Write a story in which it takes at least five trades for Person #1 to get what he wants and feel satisfied with the trade. Be as creative and comical as you like.

4. Ask a friend to read your story to make sure it flows and makes sense. Then ask your teacher to find a time for you to share your story with the class. You may choose to use props and actors to silently act out your story as you tell it.

Obsolete Jobs

Materials Needed:

- Computer with Internet access

Steps:

1. Appreciate that throughout history there have been jobs that were in high demand and then, over time, the job became extinct. For example, have you ever met anyone who worked as a lector, elevator operator, pinsetter, or lamplighter? Use your favorite Internet search engine to research jobs that are obsolete or are endangered.

2. Select 5–10 obsolete or endangered jobs that you find most interesting and unusual.

3. Create a job description in the style of a classified advertisement on a job website that gives the name of the job, what the job entailed, the qualifications that were needed to do the job, at least one photograph of someone doing the job, and an explanation of why the job is now obsolete.

4. Ask your teacher to set a time for you to share your classified ad with the class.

What's My Line?

||||||||||||||||||||||||||||||||||||||||||||||||||||||||||||||||||||||||||||||||||||||||||||||||||||||||||||||

Grade Levels: 4–5

Materials Needed:

- Computer with Internet access

Steps:

1. Between 1950 and 1967, there was a television show called *What's My Line?*. The game show had guests who had unusual jobs or careers. The contestant could only answer yes or no to questions posed. The panelists could ask only 10 questions to try to guess the job. If the job or career was not identified, the guest would explain what his or her job was and he would be declared the winner.

2. Find and watch a vintage clip of *What's My Line?* online (find a clip that does not feature celebrities).

3. Use your favorite Internet search engine to research careers or "lines of work" that are gaining in popularity and that are predicted to provide jobs in the future.

4. Identify five jobs and learn enough about the jobs to be able to answer questions as if you were currently in that profession. For example, your first game show contestant could be a desalination engineer. You would have to know what this person does, what type of education the job requires, and other details in order to answer questions like:
   a. Do you make a product?
   b. Do you provide a service?
   c. Is your job dangerous?
   d. Is your job environmentally friendly?
   e. Do you need a college degree?
   f. Is this a job in the military?
   g. Do you do this job in a foreign country?
   h. Do you operate any machinery?
   i. Do you need to major in science?
   j. Does your job help solve a problem?

5. You may need to give your classmates questions that you wrote in order for them to head in the right direction with their questioning.

6. You could help by adding an aspect of the "hangman" game to your game show. Write a blank for every letter in the job title.

7. Ask your teacher to find an appropriate time for you to play the game show with your classmates.

Chapter 31

Energy Debate Projects

Note to Teacher: In order for students to debate the forms of energy in this chapter, at least one student should each complete each of the four projects in order to have enough students for the debates. Give students the following directive:

> Before completing any of the next four projects, invite three friends to each complete one of the projects with you in order to have all of the debates happen at one time.

Nuclear Energy Debate

Materials Needed:

- Library access or computer with Internet access

Steps:

1. Use your favorite Internet search engine to help you research the parts of a debate. Be sure to define the following parts: the affirmative side, negative side, moderator, opening, first rebuttal, second rebuttal, and closing.
2. Visit the library or use the Internet to discover all you can about using nuclear energy to produce electricity. Try to answer the following questions as you research:
   a. Where are the nuclear reactors in the United States?
   b. How many nuclear power plants are in the United States?
   c. How much electricity can one nuclear power plant make?
   d. What kind of pollution does the nuclear power plant generate? How is this pollution disposed of?
   e. What are the pros to using nuclear energy?
   f. What are the cons to using nuclear energy?

3. Prepare a scripted debate that argues for and against using nuclear energy. Be sure to write the openings arguments, first rebuttal, second rebuttal, and closing arguments for each side. You can use a search engine to look for sample debate scripts to help you get started.
4. Ask two classmates to rehearse the scripted debate you wrote.
5. Ask your teacher when you and your classmates can present the debate to the class.

Coal Energy Debate

||||||||||||||||||||||||||||||||||||||||||||||||||||||||||||||||||||||||||||||||||||||||||||||||||

Grade Levels: 4–5

Materials Needed:

- Library access or computer with Internet access

Steps:

1. Use your favorite Internet search engine to help you research the parts of a debate. Be sure to define the following parts: the affirmative side, negative side, moderator, opening, first rebuttal, second rebuttal, and closing.

2. Visit the library or use the Internet to discover all you can about using coal to produce electricity. Try to answer the following questions as you research:
   a. Where is coal mined in the United States?
   b. What kinds of mining processes are used (contour mining, underground mining, etc.)?
   c. How much electricity can one coal plant make?
   d. What kind of pollution does the coal plant generate? How is this pollution disposed of?
   e. What are the pros to using coal to produce electricity?
   f. What are the cons to using coal to produce electricity?

3. Prepare a scripted debate that argues for and against using coal to produce electricity. Be sure to write the openings arguments, first rebuttal, second rebuttal, and closing arguments for each side. You can use a search engine to look for sample debate scripts to help you get started.

4. Ask two classmates to rehearse the scripted debate you wrote.

5. Ask your teacher when you and your classmates can present the debate to the class.

Oil Energy Debate

Grade Levels: 4–5

Materials Needed:

- Library access or computer with Internet access

Steps:

1. Use your favorite Internet search engine to help you research the parts of a debate. Be sure to define the following parts: the affirmative side, negative side, moderator, opening, first rebuttal, second rebuttal, and closing.

2. Visit the library or use the Internet to discover all you can about using oil to produce electricity. Try to answer the following questions as you research:
   a. Where is oil found in and around the United States?
   b. What kinds of oil extraction processes are used (drilling, fracking, etc.)?
   c. How is oil used to make electricity?
   d. What kinds of pollution does burning oil generate?
   e. What are the pros to burning oil to produce electricity?
   f. What are the cons to burning oil to produce electricity?

3. Prepare a scripted debate that argues for and against using oil to produce electricity. Be sure to write the openings arguments, first rebuttal, second rebuttal, and closing arguments for each side. You can use a search engine to look for sample debate scripts to help you get started.

4. Ask two classmates to rehearse the scripted debate you wrote.

5. Ask your teacher when you and your classmates can present the debate to the class.

Natural Gas Energy Debate

|||||||||||||||||||||||||||||||||||||||||||||||||||||||||||||||||||||||||||||||||||||||||||||||||||||||||||||||

Grade Levels: 4–5

Materials Needed:

- A large sheet of chart paper
- Library access or computer with Internet access

Steps:

1. Use your favorite Internet search engine to help you research the parts of a debate. Be sure to define the following parts: the affirmative side, negative side, moderator, opening, first rebuttal, second rebuttal, and closing.
2. Visit the library or use the Internet to discover all you can about using natural gas to produce electricity. Try to answer the following questions as you research:
   a. Where is natural gas found in and around the United States?
   b. What kinds of extraction processes are used (drilling, fracking, etc.)?
   c. How is natural gas used to make electricity?
   d. What kinds of pollution does burning natural gas generate?
   e. What are the pros to using natural gas to produce electricity?
   f. What are the cons to using natural gas to produce electricity?

3. Prepare a scripted debate that argues for and against using natural gas to produce electricity. Be sure to write the openings arguments, first rebuttal, second rebuttal, and closing arguments for each side. You can use a search engine to look for sample debate scripts to help you get started.
4. Ask two classmates to rehearse the scripted debate you wrote.
5. Ask your teacher when you and your classmates can present the debate to the class.

Chapter 32

Geography Road Trip Projects

Road Trip

Grade Levels: 4–5

Materials Needed:

- 1 United States map
- Computer with Internet access

Steps:

1. Plan a trip from Washington, DC, to Los Angeles, CA. Explore your options before deciding which mode of transportation to use.
2. Search your favorite travel site and see how long it would take and how much it would cost if you traveled by airplane, bus, or train or if you talked one of your relatives into driving you instead. Tip: If you are plotting a driving plan, then keep in mind the cost of gas, hotel rooms, and food.
3. Calculate and find the information you need and make a graph that shows your results.
4. Write a paragraph explaining which mode of transportation you would choose and why.
5. Ask your teacher to find a time for you to present your travel plan to the class.

Landforms

Grade Levels: 4–5

Materials Needed:

- Index cards
- Markers

Steps:

1. Understand that landforms are natural physical features of the Earth's surface such as valleys, mountains, plains, and hills. Research five of the following lesser known landforms: loess, atoll, fjord, alluvial fan, bajada, caldera, or cirque.

2. Create a flashcard with the name of the landform on the front and a diagram or picture and definition of the word on the other side. Research at least 10 other landforms and make flashcards of those as well.

3. Ask your teacher for a time when you can present what you learned to the class. Your teacher might wish to place these flashcards in a station to help students practice identifying landforms.

Where in the US?

Materials Needed:

- 1 United States map

Steps:

1. Find one interesting fact about each of the 50 states and present the fact to the class in a unique way.
2. Research 20 states, then write riddles that tell one fact about each state while hiding the name of the state within the sentence. For example, look at the sentences below:
   a. Mason h**id a ho**t potato in Jordy's bed. (The state's name is Idaho, and it is known for producing large amounts of potatoes.)
   b. Was that an oran**ge or gia**nt peach that you packed in my lunch? (The state's name is Georgia, and it is known for its delicious peaches.)

3. Make sure the fact is true in your sentence and underline or bold the letters that spell the state.
4. Publish your fun facts using a word processor.
5. Ask your teacher to find a time for you to share copies of your fun fact puzzles with your class.

Location Jeopardy

Grade Levels: 4–5

Materials Needed:

- 1 copy of Geography Jeopardy! (p. 221)
- Computer with Internet access

Steps:

1. Imagine you are asked to help create a geography Jeopardy! game.
2. Look at the Geography Jeopardy! sheet. The answers have been provided, but you will need to fill in the questions.
3. Use your favorite Internet search engine to discover the questions to the answers provided. Create at least 10 more questions and answers about geography for your game.
4. Ask your teacher if you can play the game in class.

Geography Jeopardy!

Q: _____

A: *This city is the home of Wall Street, Broadway, and Times Square.*

Q: _____

A: *This is a snowcapped African mountain that is 3 degrees south of the equator.*

Q: _____

A: *This is known as the Windy City.*

Q: _____

A: *This country was the birthplace of Wolfgang Amadeus Mozart.*

Q: _____

A: *This city is home to Wimbledon, Harrods, Piccadilly Circus, and the Globe Theatre.*

Q: _____

A: *This city is known as the "City of Light."*

Q: _____

A: *This country is home to the temple of Zeus and the original Olympic Stadium.*

Q: _____

A: *This is a highly populated city also known as Peking.*

Q: _____

A: *This is the city in which the Chao Phraya River meets its drainage basin.*

Q: _____

A: *This country is home to the Meiji shrine.*

Answer Keys

Which George?

Directions: Read each statement. Write either GW for George Washington or K for King George III in the blank provided.

GW Which George was sometimes considered a traitor?

K Quote from Samuel Johnson: "Of him we are much inclined to hope great things." (Samuel Johnson was the greatest English writer of his day)

GW The following quote by "Light-Horse Harry" Lee was talking about which George: "first in war, first in peace, and first in the hearts of his countrymen."

GW This George had 2 children.

K This George had 15 children.

K He hired German troops to help fight for his side.

GW He accepted help from French leaders.

K This George was married to a German princess.

GW He refused to be King of America.

K This George was the last King of America.

GW This George encouraged his soldiers to ambush, use quick speed, travel lightly, and blend in to the scenery.

K He taught his soldiers that the honorable way to fight is to march openly into battle in columns and rows, shoulder to shoulder.

GW At one time during the war he wrote, "I am wearied almost to death. I think the game is pretty near up."

K He had a House of Lords and House of Commons to make decisions for the people.

K At one time during the war he said, "I think I shall soon hear . . . loyal subjects, returning to that duty they owe to an indulgent sovereign."

Geography Jeopardy!

Q: *What is New York City?*

A: *This city is the home of Wall Street, Broadway, and Times Square.*

Q: *What is Kilimanjaro?*

A: *This is a snowcapped African mountain that is 3 degrees south of the equator.*

Q: *What is Chicago?*

A: *This is known as the Windy City.*

Q: *What is Austria?*

A: *This country was the birthplace of Wolfgang Amadeus Mozart.*

Q: *What is London?*

A: *This city is home to Wimbledon, Harrods, Piccadilly Circus, and the Globe Theater.*

Q: *What is Paris?*

A: *This city is known as the "City of Light."*

Q: *What is Greece?*

A: *This country is home to the temple of Zeus and the original Olympic Stadium.*

Q: *What is Beijing?*

A: *This is a highly populated city also known as Peking.*

Q: *What is Bangkok?*

A: *This is the city in which the Chao Phraya River meets its drainage basin.*

Q: *What is Japan?*

A: *This country is home to the Meiji shrine.*